A Whole New
YOU

A Whole New YOU

Six Steps *to* Ignite Change *for* Your Best Life

By Brett Blumenthal

amazon publishing

Published by Amazon Publishing
P.O. Box 400818
Las Vegas, NV 89140

ISBN-13: 9781612186153
ISBN-10: 1612186157

For my family,
for their love, support, and encouragement.

GOOD, BETTER, BEST. NEVER LET IT REST.

'TIL YOUR GOOD IS BETTER AND YOUR

BETTER IS BEST.

—SAINT JEROME

CONTENTS

A Personal Note to You—The Reader

BELIEVE IN TRANSFORMATION AND REINVENTION. I've morphed myself numerous times over the years, trying to become better in one area or another. I've tweaked aspects of my life that weren't quite working for me, such as developing confidence and comfort with meeting new people, and expanding my social and professional networks. I've reinvented my perspective and mindset about health and fitness. I've renewed how I approach love and relationships, even overhauled my way of thinking and perceptions of myself. It's not that I've been bored or needed some excitement—change was brought on because of a real desire to address an issue in my life, and an underlying passion for self-improvement.

The first big change I can recall was deciding I was going to take control of my health and fitness. Up until the age of seven I lived in Manhattan, where PE class was nonexistent and recess mostly included a rousing game of Red Light, Green Light, 1-2-3, an activity that by no means required great athleticism. When my family moved out to Long Island, New York, however, sports were a big part of school life.

On my first day in my new elementary school, I was herded onto the open field with my classmates to play soccer, a game with which I was completely unfamiliar. Within seconds, I was hit square in the face with the soccer ball. It hurt, but the shock and embarrassment stung much worse. From that point on, anything sports related became synonymous with humiliation. I shied away from sports, telling myself it wasn't for me.

It wasn't until college that I decided I didn't want to be judged poorly anymore for something I knew I could control. I wanted to be fit and strong, and although I might not have had talent in sports, I wanted to at least look as though I could hold my own. For the first time, I started exercising regularly. The decision was as simple as that. But I had to let go of my negative feelings from the past, make a commitment to something with which I was uncomfortable, and stick with it for the longer term.

Before long, I became an avid fan of exercise and its many benefits. I felt physically better, slept better at night, and was generally happier. I was better at managing stress and had improved focus in school. And the best outcome of my transformation was that I finally started to shed my fear of rejection and to believe in myself. I became so passionate about wellness that by the end of my freshman year, I had become a certified fitness instructor, teaching some of the most popular fitness classes on campus.

Transformations in my life have not just been related to health and fitness. After college, I started practicing architecture. Within a few years, I became frustrated by the profession: the pay was low, the industry was highly cyclical, and the career path to advancement was longer and more arduous than most. I realized that the aspects of my job that I actually enjoyed—client-relationship management, problem solving, and project management—were integral to a much higher-paying, more stable profession: management consulting.

Given that I had no business experience and came from a design profession, a transition to management consulting was somewhat unlikely. Yet, I was determined. I did research and applied a relatively rigorous process to making the change. I recognized there was a need for change; I analyzed what I wanted; I designed a vision for the future; I created a plan to make it happen; and I executed the plan with passion and determination. Within a few months, I accepted a position with PricewaterhouseCoopers Consulting (PwC).

Over the next several years as a consultant with PwC and, after business school, at Deloitte Consulting, I spent the majority of my time providing change-management services to our clients. I helped companies manage and structure the changes, the transformations, and the reinventions they faced in business so they could operate and perform better. I realized that the very process I applied to changing my career looked much like the process many businesses apply to implementing change within their organizations.

After working on over a dozen projects, big and small, and domestic as well as global, it became clear that the companies that chose to invest the time and resources to appropriately plan and manage their changes were the ones most likely to succeed. The companies that didn't put in the time or energy to plan for it, however, often faced great difficulty in making the changes work within their organizations, sometimes even failing completely.

Just as I had experienced with my own changes and reinventions on a personal level, my professional experience proved that, regardless of circumstance or situation, if change and improvement are desired, a structured process or path is required to make it a reality.

When I finally changed my career to become an author and wellness expert, I was once again reminded of the importance of process. Success was (and continues to be) dependent on a deeper understanding of myself, a constant ability to develop a clear vision, and the determination to take my vision and make it come to fruition. It excites me to finally be able to combine my passion for wellness with my extensive experience in change to bring you *A Whole New You*.

My goal in writing *A Whole New You* is to provide a simple yet effective approach to transforming any aspect of your life. Over the years, I've learned what works and what doesn't, and have become increasingly aware of factors required for success, as well as the potential roadblocks one might encounter that can debilitate even the best of intentions. Based on my personal and professional experience, as well as some of the most up-to-date research presented by experts and authors within psychology and human behavior, *A Whole New You* provides you with a detailed step-by-step guide to building the best life you can.

What inspires each of us to change can differ greatly from one person to the next, and even though your personal reinventions may differ from those of the person sitting next to you, the simple path I outline remains applicable. Whether you want to reinvent your career, your physique and health, your love life, or your emotional happiness, following the path outlined will enable you to make real change, real transformation, real reinvention.

Part I
PREPARATION

A LOOK AT PERSONAL REINVENTION

As human beings, our greatness lies not so much in being able to remake the world…as in being able to remake ourselves.

—Mahatma Gandhi

Reinvention is nothing new to us. It has existed throughout time, at every scale. We are most concerned, however, with the type of change that is most relevant to us as individuals: personal reinvention.

Let's face it: we all yearn for something better, and an attempt at personal change is what we hope will get us there.

Change versus Personal Reinvention

Throughout this book, the terms *change* and *personal reinvention* will be used often, and seemingly interchangeably. That being said, the terms differ slightly. If you look in the dictionary, *change* in its simplest form is defined as "to become different," while *reinvent* is defined as "to remake or redo completely." The difference between these terms basically comes down to semantics. For the sake of clarity, however, you can think about it in this way: it is all about scale. A change can be singular, or focused on one habit or characteristic. Personal reinvention, however, tends to require many changes and is much larger in scale. Essentially, you will make many changes that will culminate in a personal reinvention.

Why We Change

Whether we realize it or not, many of us change or reinvent quite frequently, modifying our behaviors and our thoughts in order to adjust to situations and life circumstances as they occur. As a matter of fact, most would argue that change is good for us: it allows us to adapt, to grow, and to flourish. When we stop changing, however, we run the risk of becoming stagnant and getting stuck. Change is a necessary component of living to our full potential, being the best we can be, and taking advantage of all that life has to offer.

> Your life does not get better by chance, it gets better by change.
>
> —*Jim Rohn*

When we embark on making change, it may appear that we do so for many different reasons. We reinvent careers because we don't like the type of work we do or the industry we've chosen. We reinvent our personality so we can appear more outgoing or sociable. We reinvent our health so we can prevent—or possibly even help eliminate—disease. But if you get to the very core of all of these personal reinventions, our desire to change comes down to one very simple yet important mission: to be happy.

In Gretchen Rubin's *The Happiness Project*, the author shares her experiences and thoughts about her pursuit of a happier life through a project that extends over the course of a year. She openly admits to her readers that she isn't unhappy but she thinks she could be happier. She explains that her project isn't so much about *overcoming unhappiness* as it is about *maximizing happiness* so she can be the happiest she can be—not only for herself but for her family, friends, and even the world.

And so if we continually strive to be happier, even at a marginal level, it ultimately drives our interest in change and personal reinvention.

> *Recently, Sam went through a career reinvention. In school he had studied English, but when he graduated, he was lured into a job in pharmaceutical sales. He had been working in the industry for over ten years and was making very good money, but when he and his wife had a baby, he decided to make a change.*
>
> *Sam's job in pharmaceutical sales required extensive travel, so he accepted a position as a journalist with a major Boston newspaper so he could spend more time at home. This seemed like a logical reason to change careers.*

One afternoon, Sam and I discussed his new job. I asked, "The new job must pay a great deal less than what you were making before, no?" He flatly agreed. I then asked if this was an issue for him and his family. He explained that although money was tighter, he wanted to be at home. Raising his newborn son with his wife was important, and he didn't want to miss out on that experience. I asked if there was any way he could have worked something out with his previous company to reduce the travel. He confessed that he actually knew other employees who had managed to cut back their travel schedules, but it seemed like too much of a hassle.

This made me ask, "Did you like your job?" His response was an unenthusiastic "It paid really well." I pushed further: "But did you like *your job? Were you happy going to work and doing what you did?" He thought for a moment and confided that he didn't. As a matter of fact, until the baby was born, he had wanted to leave for over a year, but felt the money was too good to warrant the change.*

"Are you happy with your job now*?" I asked. He replied that he was and that he had always dreamed of being a writer. He went on to explain how much he now loved going to work. Finally, I inquired, "Do you have to travel?" He admitted he did, but somehow it didn't bother him.*

On the surface, Sam's decision to change careers stemmed from a logistical desire to be at home more often for his family and to travel less. But a deeper look revealed that the change was a result of a desire for greater happiness. Yes, he still wanted to be home more for his family, but travel wasn't the main driver. We know this because (1) he likely could have changed his travel schedule with his first job; (2) he admitted that he didn't like his job and wanted to change before the baby arrived; and (3) he still was required to travel with his new job and yet didn't really mind it. Happiness in his career was the real, deeper reason for the change.

WHEN WE CHANGE

Although there are times when change is foisted upon us, *choosing* to change is what we are most concerned with throughout this book. When we choose to change or reinvent ourselves, we do so as a result of what life brings us, expected or unexpected. When we experience changes to our environment or our circumstances, or we experience life-changing events, we may be prompted to reflect on our life and to think about ways we could make it better.

This ultimately creates a spark that motivates us to reinvent for tomorrow. Sometimes we refer to this as having an "epiphany" or an "Aha! moment." Although these realizations can occur at any time, they generally emerge as a result of one of the following three types of life experiences we typically encounter throughout our lifetime.

LIFE TRANSITIONS

> When one door closes, another opens...
>
> —*Alexander Graham Bell*

One of the most common times we are inspired to make change is when one chapter of our life ends and another begins. These life transitions often coincide with changes to our environment, living conditions, and potential social or familial situations. Typical examples include the transition from high school to college, from college to starting our first job, from single status to married, from childlessness to parenthood, or from employee to retiree. All of these shifts from one chapter to another represent a change in our circumstances that may require some form of adaptation, either by necessity or by choice.

These life transitions present natural opportunities to modify our behavior or thought processes. And if we are leaving an especially distasteful or difficult stage in life, we may be even more motivated to wipe the slate clean, develop a new persona, and enter our new chapter with a fresh start.

The personal desire for change I had during the transition from high school to college isn't so uncommon. Studies show that many people rank their adolescent years as the worst. They are the most fragile yet growth-oriented times of our lives. We are still trying to figure out who we are and what we want. And we are eager to establish our independence and claim our own identity.

Jane's parents were immigrants from China and tended to keep to themselves. She was taught that her studies were very important and although she played the violin and performed in the school's orchestra, she didn't have many opportunities to socialize outside of school. As a result, she was perceived as boring and antisocial. As Jane finished her last year of high school, she desperately looked forward to escaping her status as a shy and quiet person, to earn a more sociable and outgoing reputation.

Jane knew college would provide a whole new environment away from her social and familial norms. She was excited to meet new people, find new activities to get involved in, and establish a reputation that was completely unique and separate from the one she had as a high school student. Although she was brought up to be quiet, Jane felt deep down that she was much more social and outgoing than was tolerated by her parents. As a result, she was inspired to change and become the person she wanted to be.

Psychologically, Jane found it much less intimidating to take on a new persona in college. It was unfamiliar, but it was much easier to establish a new identity in a new place rather than trying to convert or reformulate an existing reputation with those individuals who already knew her.

When Jane arrived at college, she demonstrated a more extroverted side, enabling her to make friends easily. She signed up for extracurricular activities, and even ran for student office. Since no one had known her previously, she was able to establish a new social norm. The new people she met didn't know the old Jane, quiet and shy; they only knew her as the more outgoing person she now presented herself to be.

As you can see, life transitions present us with a very natural way to make change. By providing us with a new set of circumstances, we have less to overcome in resetting our norm, and so it feels more manageable, even simpler.

LIFE-CHANGING EVENTS

> A thought, even a possibility, can shatter and transform us.
>
> —*Friedrich Nietzsche*

Another typical time for personal reinvention is when we go through an event or a series of events that change our perspective or bring us enlightenment. A new perspective may force us to examine our life and discover that we aren't very happy or don't feel very fulfilled. As a result, it causes us to evaluate what would really bring us happiness, revealing opportunities for change. We often call these "life-changing events."

Andy had a very successful career on Wall Street. When he was young, he put everything into his job and into making money. As he got older, however, this narrow focus on work eventually took a toll on other aspects of his life. He gained fifty pounds and started to have health issues due to the tremendous amount of travel and entertaining he did with clients. Further, he spent very little time with his family, often missing important milestones of his children.

Andy gained new perspective, however, after the life-changing events of September 11, 2001. For years Andy had visited dozens of money management firms in and around the Wall Street area, and had walked through the World Trade Center countless times. The morning of the attacks, however, he was fortunate to be on the road traveling. Yet the events of that day dramatically impacted him. In watching them unfold, he quickly realized that completely unforeseen circumstances could greatly affect his life, as well as the lives of those he loves. It made him reevaluate what was truly important to him.

The second event occurred on May 1, 2010. Andy and his family stood at the intersection of Forty-Fifth Street and Broadway in New York City, a mere fifteen feet from a car packed with explosives. The car was set to explode at the very time Andy, his wife, and his kids were there. Fortunately, the explosives never went off, but it once again reaffirmed to Andy that life is short and it is important to live focused on genuine value, not on money.

After the events of 9/11, Andy started to reinvent his life by designing the lifestyle he wanted. That meant setting goals to get out of corporate America and to make his family the number one priority. Today, Andy works out of his house most days of the week. He has addressed his health issues, making his health and spirituality priorities. He even started a health and wellness company to help individuals live their healthiest. Because of his strong desire to live a life of value, Andy also started a consulting company to help others grow their own businesses. Finally, he and his family enjoy a much more fulfilling and rewarding life together. Andy is now present for the milestones and events that are important in his children's lives and can enjoy a deeper and more loving relationship with his wife. In short, Andy is much happier and is living the lifestyle he truly wants. His gained perspective gave him a new lease on life.

Reinventions that result from gained perspective or a heightened level of awareness are generally less predictable than those that come during a life transition. They are more exemplary of the "Aha! moment" or "epiphany" mentioned earlier. They are often due to unexpected events that cause us to see things differently from how we may have seen them previously.

Loss or Misfortune

> Every adversity, every failure, every heartache carries with it the seed of an equal or greater benefit.
>
> —*Napoleon Hill*

The third and final type of life experience that may prompt us to go through a personal reinvention is when we experience loss or misfortune. In these situations we are dealing with circumstances over which we have little to no control. For instance, we may lose our spouse through a divorce, we may lose our job through a layoff, we may lose a friend or loved one to death, or we may even lose our health through an accident or the onset of disease. Loss in any format can create a large void, and as a result, may force us to search for something better or to fill the hole that has developed. In these cases, a personal reinvention can be a form of healing, or a way of dealing with the pain and hurt.

Throughout her life, Lisa attracted needy people. Friends, family members, colleagues, and even romantic partners all leaned heavily on Lisa, relying on her to take care of the messes they created. She spent so much time and energy helping everyone around her and dealing with their problems and issues that she had little to no time for herself. She was exhausted, and in neglecting her own health and wellbeing, Lisa started to feel depressed, gain weight, and notice a series of health issues percolating.

The stress and lack of self-care Lisa experienced finally caused her to have a breakdown that required hospitalization. After spending two weeks recovering, she knew things had to change. She knew she couldn't continue doing everything for everyone else, neglecting her own health, happiness, and needs in the process. After her release from the hospital, she sought help from a therapist. The therapist helped her to understand that she desperately needed to draw boundaries and learn to say no. Within a month, Lisa started to reprioritize so she could take time for herself and her needs before attending to those of everyone else.

Over a month or so, Lisa eventually began to feel better physically and mentally. She learned to identify the behaviors that caused her to attract needy individuals. And by working on modifying those behaviors, Lisa began to minimize the unhealthy relationships in her life. She instead started to attract those who were healthier and more supportive. Lisa felt reborn. She felt happier and healthier, and was finally able to really enjoy life and have fun.

In Lisa's situation, her loss in health provided her with a wake-up call. Once we can get past the pain, hurt, or feelings of loss or misfortune, we may be inspired to question what we want, what we hope for from our relationships, how we want to age, or what we want or need to do to ultimately achieve happiness. Reinvention inspired by loss can be dramatically life-changing.

WAYS WE CHANGE: DIMENSIONS OF WELL-BEING

Personal reinvention can occur on a multitude of levels, ranging from dramatic change resulting in a full transformation to change that is less extreme and focuses on the modification of a very specific component of life. Regardless, personal reinventions tend to include changes associated with one or more *dimensions of well-being*.

Dimensions of well-being include those aspects of our life that directly contribute to our ability to be happy. These dimensions can be categorized into the following: career, physical, social, emotional, intellectual, and spiritual (see the "Dimensions of Well-Being" figure on page 13). Achieving an optimal state of well-being—and thus, happiness—is dependent on our behaviors, our thoughts, and our choices within each of these areas. Each of these six dimensions can be broken down further into subcategories, but for the sake of simplicity, we'll focus on these overarching themes as we move forward throughout the book.

You may find that certain dimensions feel more important to you than others. Each of us is unique, and what is deemed valuable can vary greatly from person to person. That said, whether you think you value all the following dimensions of well-being or not, realize that each plays some factor in your ability to be happy—even if at a lower level than others.

DIMENSIONS OF WELL-BEING

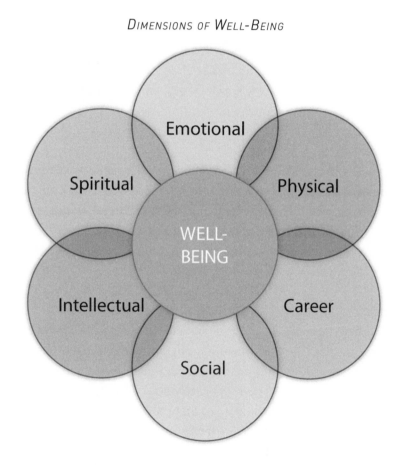

CAREER WELL-BEING

In a 2008 study by the Organization for Economic Cooperation and Development, it was found that Americans work an average of thirty-five hours per week. Given that this represents more than 30 percent of our time while we are awake, it is safe to say that what we do for work has a tremendous impact on our happiness. With the most recent economic downturn, we've seen countless individuals reinvent their careers in order to accommodate the high rate of unemployment and difficult job market. When job markets are strong, however, individuals may embark on a career reinvention purely because they don't find their current job or career fulfilling or rewarding. Regardless of the motivation, these reinventions can be as minor as a lateral shift in role or job description within a particular industry, or much more robust, such as a full-blown switch to a completely different career in a different industry.

PHYSICAL WELL-BEING

Personal reinventions pertaining to physical well-being occur when we make positive change to our overall physical health. This can involve weight loss (a $60 billion industry in the United States), changing how and what we eat, improving our level of fitness, or even more drastic changes in order to improve certain medical conditions. We tend to embark on this kind of change either because we have a desire to improve our health as an act of prevention or because we have a desire to fight a diagnosis of disease we may already have.

SOCIAL WELL-BEING

Social well-being focuses on how we socialize and interact with others and our behavior and personality within relationships. Personal reinventions within this dimension can extend to all types of relationships, including those with acquaintances, colleagues, friends, or family members, and even romantic partners. At a high level, changes might include working on body language to be more approachable, such as looking people in the eye, keeping arms at one's side instead of crossed, and leaning in when speaking to another individual. Or it could include deeper modifications, such as developing a level of comfort with meeting new people, acting more confident, and developing better listening skills. Going even further, work may be done on foundational behaviors such as forming, maintaining, and acting within relationships. At this level, trust, commitment, security, openness, honesty, and other qualities might be addressed in order to create relationships that are more meaningful and rewarding.

EMOTIONAL WELL-BEING

In contrast to social well-being, which focuses on attaining happiness through our relationships with others, emotional well-being focuses on our ability to attain happiness within ourselves. A personal reinvention in this dimension can address internal character, behaviors, reactions, emotions, thoughts, and self-perceptions. As we grow and gain experience, we begin to look at ourselves in specific ways. We also develop certain ways of thinking, and potentially a hardened perspective, or certain emotional and behavioral responses to typical situations. A personal reinvention that addresses our emotional well-being requires an adjustment to these behaviors and thoughts. It may involve diminishing anger or resentment. It might involve developing patience, sympathy, compassion, and understanding. Or in many cases it may involve cultivating a more positive outlook, building self-esteem and self-confidence, and developing a strong sense of self. This type of reinvention, in particular, benefits from deeper analysis of who we are and why we are the way we are, so we can learn from the past and build a happier, more rewarding future.

INTELLECTUAL WELL-BEING

Although personal reinventions around intellectual well-being are probably less common than those within other dimensions of well-being, they still warrant a brief discussion here. Our intellectual well-being relies on the happiness we get from developing personal interests, using our creativity, and engaging our minds. Changes can involve learning new hobbies, growing intellectually, and challenging the mind in order to ward off age-related disease or memory loss. For instance, you might develop deeper passions and pursuits, such as photography or dance. Or changes might involve stimulating your intellect and keeping your mind sharp and youthful by reading more, through puzzles or games such as sudoku or crossword puzzles, or by tapping into your creativity. And finally, a reinvention in this dimension might include building knowledge or skill sets, and studying subjects of interest, either independently or within an academic environment.

SPIRITUAL WELL-BEING

Finally, one of the most complicated and provocative personal reinventions one can make is within the dimension of spiritual well-being. This involves a much more intricate and deeper transformation, one that is highly emotional and transcendental. This kind of transformation is usually all-encompassing and can involve changes within other dimensions of well-being as well. It generally requires deep introspection, a tremendous amount of emotional and psychological work, and great amounts of energy and time. Personal reinvention within the dimension of spirituality is often associated with shifts in philosophy, moral beliefs, and altruistic concerns. And although it can involve an overhaul of many facets of one's life, these reinventions can surprisingly stem from the simplest and least predictable, yet most impactful, moments in our life.

Each dimension of well-being contributes to our overall happiness. As you begin the journey on your path to personal reinvention, you may discover that one or more of these dimensions warrant change. Be open to the possibilities of reinvention throughout all dimensions, but pay close attention to what your heart and mind tell you. Only you know what kind of change is most relevant and important to you.

A LOOK AT PERSONAL REINVENTION

THERE ARE THREE CONSTANTS IN LIFE…CHANGE, CHOICE, AND PRINCIPLES.

—*STEPHEN R. COVEY*

CHANGE HAS BEEN A LONG-DISCUSSED topic on many fronts and within many circles. Although we can't cover centuries' worth of research and documentation on change here, highlighting some of the most current work and discussions that have influenced or supported what is presented on the following pages may be valuable.

Although some of these authors discuss change in the context of business, society, or politics, many of their points can be applied at a personal level. My mission in sharing these summaries with you is to distill some of the key points each author presents, so that the principles and research can be applied to your own personal reinvention and attempts at change.

THE POWER OF HABIT

In *The Power of Habit: Why We Do What We Do in Life and Business*, Charles Duhigg looks at the habits of individuals, organizations, and societies, and tries to explain the science and behavioral psychology of how habits work. He writes, "When a habit emerges, the brain stops fully participating in decision-making." He tells us that habits make up about 40 percent of our daily routine, and in order to change them, we have to understand what he calls the "habit loop."

The habit loop consists of a cue or trigger, a routine, and a reward. Duhigg provides a personal example where at 3:00 p.m. every day he would go to his cafeteria and buy a cookie. Over time, this ultimately led to his gaining weight. Curious about what was at the heart of the weight gain, he conducted a few experiments and realized that his cue was the time of day (3:00 p.m.), his routine was a trip to the cafeteria to purchase a cookie, and surprisingly, the reward was socialization with friends and colleagues—not the taste of the cookie itself. As a result, he saw an opportunity to change the overall habit by tweaking specific components of the habit loop. He decided to maintain the reward of socialization, while modifying the less healthy routine of purchasing and eating a cookie. At 3:00 p.m., instead of going to the cafeteria for a cookie, Duhigg started to find ways to socialize within his office environment and avoid the cafeteria altogether. He soon found his craving for the cookie had disappeared.

Changing a habit may not always be about changing the routine. It could involve changing or eliminating the cue or replacing an unhealthy reward with one that is healthier. In short, to stop or modify a bad or unwanted habit, you must understand the habit loop, and identify what part of it is creating unwanted results. You can then redesign it (or stop it altogether) so that new, healthier habits can form.

> **How It Applies to Your Path:** Your personal reinvention will inevitably require making modifications to habits, behaviors, and thought processes. As you progress on your path, be mindful of the habit loops you have created in your life. For those habit loops that seem to result in negative consequences (such as weight gain, in Duhigg's example), you'll want to investigate which part of the loop is to blame. You'll then want to identify what you can do to modify your habit loop to produce more favorable behaviors or results. This will be discussed more specifically in **Stage 5: Make It Happen.**

SWITCH

In *Switch: How to Change Things When Change Is Hard*, Chip and Dan Heath discuss a model for making change in which it is crucial to appeal to the two sides of our mind—the rational side and the emotional side—while providing a clear, unobstructed path on which change can be made.

Borrowing from an analogy presented in Jonathan Haidt's *The Happiness Hypothesis*, the Heath brothers label the rational side of our brains the "Rider" and the emotional side the "Elephant." The rational side, or Rider, knows *why* it should change; however, the emotional side, or Elephant, prefers comfort and routine, and as a result, needs motivation to *want* to change. Using this metaphor, they go on to explain that the small Rider sits on top of the big Elephant, attempting to control and guide it. Yet, if there is disagreement between the two, the Rider exhausts itself trying to get the big Elephant to listen. In this situation, the Elephant ultimately wins due to its sheer strength and size. In other words, our emotional side tends to win over our rational side because it is much stronger when there is misalignment between the two.

This need to appeal to both sides of our brain can easily be demonstrated when we go on a diet. Our Rider, or rational side, will understand the logical benefits of eating healthily and why unhealthy food is bad for us. Thus, it will try to keep our Elephant, or emotional side, from giving in to cravings. Our Elephant, however, is much stronger, and unless it is motivated to stick with the diet plan, it will eventually cause us to give in to the cravings our Rider tries to avoid. When embarking on change, you can count on the Rider to plan and direct, but in the end you need to motivate the Elephant to *want* to follow the plan.

Once you've gotten both your Rider and Elephant engaged in the process, the third piece of the Heath brothers' philosophy—"shape the path"—can be addressed. In short, shaping the path means finding ways to make the process of change easier for both the Rider and the Elephant, so that it is more likely to stick. For the Rider, you want to provide a clear and simple process for it to follow, and for the Elephant, you want to remove any obstacles that might come into its path. Obstacles can present themselves in different ways: via environmental circumstances, people, bad habits, or an inability to keep motivation levels high. Regardless of what the obstacles are, shaping the path aims to remove them, or at least minimize them so that the path to change is easier.

How It Applies to Your Path: Throughout the process outlined, you will engage both your rational (Rider) and emotional (Elephant) sides. Both are very important and need to be considered. Generally, the rational side of why you might want to change is clear, but the *wanting* of the emotional side may not be. To help, you'll want to ask yourself the following questions throughout the process: Am I motivated to do this? Do I want to accomplish this goal? How can I become more motivated?

When it comes to shaping your path, the steps you take and activities you do throughout the process will encourage simplifying change so it is most likely to stick. Additionally, pay attention to the roadblocks discussed so you can be mindful of the typical obstacles that present themselves at each stage of your path to personal reinvention.

Mindset

In *Mindset: The New Psychology of Success*, psychologist Carol Dweck discusses how our mindset is what allows us to be successful or holds us back. She goes on to explain that we have either a *fixed mindset* or a *growth mindset*.

The *fixed mindset* is one in which people believe that their basic qualities, such as intelligence or talent, are fixed traits. Instead of trying to develop these traits, they tend to "document" them. They also believe their talent(s) will carry them toward success, and thus they rely heavily on what already is. As a result, they don't put much effort or work into strengthening their talents or strengths, or for that matter, building any new ones.

On the other hand, the *growth mindset* is one in which people believe they can continually develop their abilities through dedication and hard work. In this case, the intellect and the talent are the foundation from which one can grow and become stronger. Dweck argues that this mindset creates a love of learning and resilience essential to accomplishment.

> **How It Applies to Your Path:** A growth mindset will be required in order for you to believe you are capable of making change. If you maintain a fixed mindset, change won't be possible.
>
> Through the self-discovery process during **Stage 2: Discover Yourself,** you'll do a variety of activities to uncover your strengths, your weaknesses, your accomplishments, your failures, and even your fears. All of your past experiences will play a role in helping you to change and create the personal reinvention you desire. When uncovering seemingly negative experiences, avoid dismissing them or feeling bad about them. Instead, try to learn from them. If you believe you are limited by past negative experiences, you are staying in a fixed mindset. If, however, you learn from past mistakes and believe you can push through fear and negativity, you will encourage a growth mindset.

THE 7 HABITS OF HIGHLY EFFECTIVE PEOPLE

The 7 Habits of Highly Effective People is an old standby in the personal development and self-help genre of publications. Author Stephen R. Covey explains that habits are the intersection of knowledge (what to, why to), skills (how to), and desire (want to). Throughout the text you can find some overlap with both Charles Duhigg's habit loop and the Heath brothers' change model of the Rider, the Elephant, and shaping the path. Stephen Covey's differentiation, however, is that instead of discussing the process, he gets to the heart of the specific habits and personal characteristics that make people effective.

Habits 1, 2, and 3 are focused on self-mastery. Habits 4, 5, and 6 are more specific to effectiveness with others, and Habit 7 focuses on bringing everything together so you can work toward continuous improvement. All are valuable, but Habits 1, 2, and 3 are most relevant to the work you'll be doing.

Habit 1 is "Be Proactive." This means taking responsibility for your life to make things happen instead of waiting for them to happen. It also means that you should take ownership of your behaviors, thoughts, and actions instead of blaming them on your circumstances or other people.

Habit 2 is "Begin with the End in Mind." This habit gets into visualizing your life as if you were at the end of it. Covey asks such questions as: "What would you want to have accomplished by the end of your life?" and "What would you want to be said at your funeral?" Thinking with the "end in mind" means forgetting about your perceived limitations of today and instead getting to the heart of your values and how you would have wanted to live your life if it were at its end. This enables you to focus on developing a vision for the future and the possibilities of tomorrow instead of getting stuck in the past.

Habit 3 is "Put First Things First." This habit relies on Habits 1 and 2 and prioritizing around your principles. It encourages living life and making decisions predicated on your values and what is truly important to you as an individual instead of on things that are unimportant, what other people expect or want, or things that are out of alignment with who you really are.

How It Applies to Your Path: All three habits are essential to your ability to complete your path to personal reinvention. To some extent, they transcend each stage. More specifically, however, they apply as follows: In **Stage 2: Discover Yourself**, you will do a lot of work to gain a deeper understanding of your values. This will give you insight that will allow you to have a "Put First Things First" mentality. Also, within this stage you'll be asked to write your mission statement, which requires that you think with "the end in mind." In **Stage 4: Create the Plan** and **Stage 5: Make It Happen**, you will need to be proactive and take responsibility for your actions so you can progress forward. This ultimately supports Stephen Covey's Habit 1, "Be Proactive."

There are many other books and publications on the topic of change and personal development, but the examples discussed provide concepts that are highly applicable and relevant to what you'll be doing throughout *A Whole New You*. If you are interested in other resources around the topics of change, personal reinvention, self-development, and happiness, consult the resources listed at the end of this book.

HOW TO USE THIS BOOK

WITHOUT CONTINUAL GROWTH AND PROGRESS, SUCH WORDS AS IMPROVEMENT, ACHIEVEMENT, AND SUCCESS HAVE NO MEANING.

—BENJAMIN FRANKLIN

N O DOUBT, CHANGE IS HARD. If it were easy, we'd all be able to lose weight at the drop of a hat; would set and reach our goals effortlessly; would be the perfect friend, spouse, or family member at all times; and would continually be successful and happy. But change is indeed difficult. As we learned with the Heath brothers' Rider and Elephant metaphor, the difficulty in making change lies in the fact that we not only need to understand why the change is good for us and how to proceed making it, but that we also need to maintain a high level of motivation to want to make the change. We need to continually engage both sides of our brains—the rational (Rider) and the emotional (Elephant).

In *Switch*, the Heath brothers go on to describe the Rider as a long-term planner who deliberates and analyzes while the Elephant looks for instant gratification, often responding to emotional impulses. The Rider is the thinker, and the Elephant is the doer. The Rider has the logical understanding while the Elephant has the motivation. The Rider attempts to lead, but the Elephant must follow. Change couldn't happen without the both of them; they work in synergy.

YOUR PATH TO PERSONAL REINVENTION

In Part II, you will engage both sides of the mind to ensure that your efforts to make change are successful. Each stage presented plays an important role and includes (1) an explanation as to why the stage is important; (2) steps, tasks, and activities to complete; (3) key success factors important to the stage; and (4) typical roadblocks you might encounter and how to overcome them.

YOUR PATH TO PERSONAL REINVENTION

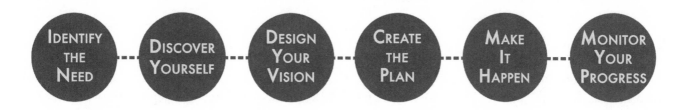

STAGE 1: IDENTIFY THE NEED

The first stage is to identify a need or desire for change. You will learn about the types of signs you might experience and how to recognize them in your own life. And you will learn to understand which dimensions of well-being are of the biggest concern to you.

STAGE 2: DISCOVER YOURSELF

In Stage 2 you will develop strong self-awareness. In order to change your behaviors, thoughts, and emotional responses, you need to have a deep understanding of yourself, your past, and why you are the way you are. You will go through a variety of exercises and activities to help you identify your values, strengths and weaknesses, accomplishments and failures, passions, fears, motivators, and more, all of which will help you in creating a vision that is most authentic to you and what you want.

STAGE 3: DESIGN YOUR VISION

Utilizing the work you did during Stages 1 and 2, you will design your vision for your future. Your vision will provide you with the direction you need to make meaningful change toward your personal reinvention.

STAGE 4: CREATE THE PLAN

In Stage 4 you'll create a plan that will be instrumental to achieving the vision you developed in Stage 3. You will go through several activities to guide you in developing and prioritizing end goals, milestones, and action steps, all of which will be the basis for your plan to make the changes you want. You'll also set target dates for completion and devise an appropriate way to reward and celebrate your accomplishments.

STAGE 5: MAKE IT HAPPEN

In Stage 5 you'll learn how to most effectively put your plan into action so you can achieve all the goals you identified in Stage 4. You'll discover how to overcome potential roadblocks and how to keep motivation levels high throughout the process.

STAGE 6: MONITOR YOUR PROGRESS

As you make changes and follow your plan, it will be important to monitor your progress. This allows you to make modifications to your plan in a timely manner so you can quickly adjust things when they aren't working. Monitoring your progress will also enable you to identify if and when changes in your environment, relationships, or other circumstances are impacting you and your efforts so that you can make adjustments accordingly.

FOLLOWING THE PATH

There is great importance in following the path in the order it is presented. Each stage represents a vital role to the process of change. Although it might be tempting to skip one or more of the six stages, or even the steps within each, doing so would do a great disservice to you and your efforts.

Stage 1: Identify the Need is vital to recognizing the signs that you have a desire for change. Without this recognition you won't be able to effectively go through **Stage 2: Discover Yourself** to better understand why this desire is presenting itself. Without self-discovery you won't be able to craft a meaningful vision in **Stage 3: Design Your Vision**. And without a vision you can't effectively go on to **Stage 4: Create the Plan**. Finally, without a plan, there's nothing to put into action in **Stage 5: Make It Happen**. Although **Stage 6: Monitor Your Progress** will require you to go back and revise some of the work you did in previous stages, following the first five stages in progression is going to make your personal reinvention much more sound and successful. Skipping any of them, however, could result in change that is misguided.

Take your time as you go through the process and be as thorough as possible. If change is truly important to you, you owe it to yourself to give it the time it requires for true success. Spending the time you need will not only produce a better end result, but your personal reinvention will also be a true reflection of who you are and what you want, making it much more likely to stick. Lastly, by following the path outlined and going through each of the exercises presented, you will build enthusiasm, passion, and true momentum toward keeping your emotional side engaged in order to successfully achieve your goals.

A Friendly Recommendation

You are probably very excited about the changes you want to make, and your personal reinvention. That said, you might find it helpful to first read through all of Part II once before formally doing any of the work outlined at each stage. Part II is extremely activity oriented and requires quite a bit of work. Reading through all of Part II first may give you time to digest what will be asked of you so you can progress through the process most effectively.

This is your journey, however, so you ultimately need to do what is best for you. If reading through Part II in its entirety seems discouraging, then by all means, don't do so. This book is meant to educate, inspire, and empower you, not frustrate you.

Keep a Journal

Since Part II will require you to do a lot of exercises and activities, I recommend that you start a personal reinvention journal. Documenting your process will be extremely helpful and provides numerous benefits:

- **It Makes It More Official:** Putting thoughts, feelings, and reactions down in writing makes them seem more formal, official, and permanent. On the other hand, keeping them purely in your mind makes it easy for them to leave as quickly as they came. Your journal will act as an official record so that your work is meaningfully captured. It allows you to treat the process more seriously and gives you an opportunity to reference your inner thoughts and emotions later if you need to.

- **It Helps You Keep Track:** Keeping a journal provides a method for tracking progress. There is nothing more rewarding than documenting your plan, reviewing your progress, and seeing how you are able to successfully achieve your goals. This will keep you inspired and give you a feeling of continued success as you go through your journey.

- **It Aids Expression:** When we write in a journal, we are forced to articulate ourselves in a meaningful and understandable way. Further, the simple act of writing slows down our response time, encouraging deeper thought and more expansive and thorough expression.

- **It Makes You More Observant:** Keeping a journal gives us reason to look around and observe what is going on around us and in our environment. It helps us to think about things more carefully and seriously than we might otherwise.

- **It Makes You Accountable:** Finally, documenting your process encourages accountability. With every goal, milestone, and action step you create, you'll feel more responsible in committing to them and completing them.

Part III: The New You Journal is filled with templates for each activity and exercise you are asked to complete in Part II. Although you can use them as they are in the book, I recommend that you reference them as templates and re-create them in a separate journal (so you can have more space for writing). Feel free to photocopy any of the templates, scan them, or transfer them to an electronic format—whatever you feel is best suited to how you want to work and maintain your written log. If you would like to download the templates in a PDF format, please visit www.sheerbalance.com/a-whole-new-you/tools-and-forms/.

Part II

YOUR PATH TO
PERSONAL
REINVENTION

STAGE 1: IDENTIFY THE NEED

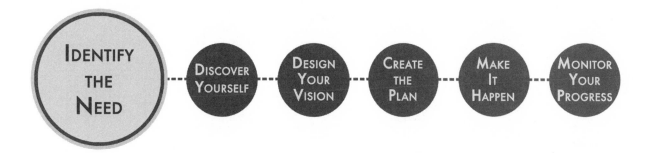

THE ONLY REAL VALUABLE THING IS INTUITION.

—ALBERT EINSTEIN

OUR DESIRE TO CHANGE IS usually triggered by some type of dissatisfaction we experience within one or more dimensions of well-being. We receive signs that tell us that something about our current situation or way of living isn't sustainable for the future, isn't driving us toward greater happiness, or isn't allowing us to be at our best.

> *Charlene was going through a seemingly difficult time over several months. She felt stressed at work but was also experiencing many negative emotions in other areas of her life. She lacked energy for things she used to look forward to, she had little to no interest in seeing friends, and she felt generally sad most of the time. Charlene's emotions were all over the map. She knew something needed to change.*

In order to change her situation, Charlene needed to acknowledge her emotions as well as understand them. She needed to identify what was causing her feelings so she could effectively make a plan to address them and to improve her circumstances.

Sometimes the signs are quite obvious, while at other times they may be subtler. And sometimes the signs are there, but it is difficult to decipher their root cause. Learning to identify that change is needed is extremely important, but so is understanding *why*. This is a crucial first step in constructing the life you want.

As we discussed in Part I, change depends on your ability to engage both the emotional and the rational sides of your brain. Stage 1 specifically engages your emotional side. Your feelings, emotions, reactions, and natural responses to your situations or circumstances provide you with a wealth of information. They tell you that change is needed. They provide you with insight as to how you'd like things to be different. And, they help to ignite the passion within to make it happen. Tapping into these deeper emotions is essential to providing you with the desire to create a better life for yourself and to change things for the future.

STAGE 1 ACTION STEPS

Stage 1 focuses on heightening your awareness of the signs that may indicate change is in order.

STEP 1: UNDERSTAND THE TYPES OF SIGNS

As we discussed in Part I, our ability to find happiness is closely tied to various dimensions of well-being. Each dimension, in its own unique way, provides opportunities for us to gauge our level of contentment or satisfaction within that specific dimension. If we are dissatisfied, then that dimension of well-being might be a target area within which to reinvent or change.

To effectively recognize signs of needed change, it's essential to be perceptive about what is happening around you, and how you are responding mentally, physically, and emotionally. It means observing and listening for clues that give you insight into when something is working and when something isn't. Fine-tuning this ability is crucial.

A need for change often shows itself by way of one of three types of signs: rational, physical, or emotional. *Rational signs* tend to be fact-based, with data present that something isn't right (e.g., an annual physical that reveals high cholesterol or high blood pressure). *Physical signs* are a result of how we respond physically to various situations or circumstances (e.g., we *experience* stress or pain). And finally, *emotional signs* are much more qualitative and are a result of our feelings and emotional responses to our environment and experiences within it.

RATIONAL SIGNS

Rational signs are very easy to see and understand, and tend to be relatively indisputable. They are apparent in situations where there is very little room for interpretation and are based more on fact than on feeling. Some dimensions of well-being are more prone to rational signs than others. For instance:

CAREER WELL-BEING

- Your salary is below your market value.

- You are putting in a lot of overtime, working ten to twelve hours per day.

- There are not enough employees at your company to do the work.

- There is no upward mobility in your current career or job.

Physical Well-Being

- Your body mass index (BMI) is too high.

- You have high blood pressure.

- You don't exercise.

- You smoke.

- You drink excessively.

- You have a debilitating disease.

- You are dependent on medication to keep vitals (e.g., blood pressure) in check.

Social Well-Being

- You constantly fight with your partner.

- You see friends or family on a highly irregular basis.

- You don't get along with family members.

- Your relationships are superficial and lack deeper connections.

Intellectual Well-Being

- You are constantly forgetting things at work and at home.

- You find everyday problem solving, such as basic arithmetic, difficult.

- You constantly struggle to find the words you want to use when speaking.

- You are unaware or out of touch with what is happening around you.

- You lack creative outlets or hobbies.

Although rational signs are obviously clear, they have a drawback: they don't necessarily tap into our emotional side or motivate us to make change. For instance, let's say Tom has a BMI of 35. According to commonly held standards, a BMI over 25 is an indication that an individual is overweight, while a BMI of 35 or higher is an indication that an individual is obese. Clearly, with a BMI of 35, Tom is obese, and as a result, *should* want to lose weight. Yet that alone may not motivate him to *want* to lose weight. By solely relying on rational signs, our emotional side may not be engaged, and so, an attempt to change is less likely to stick.

PHYSICAL SIGNS

Physical signs, too, are obvious and somewhat indisputable. They reveal themselves through physical symptoms that are unpleasant or uncomfortable, and—though not always—can be connected to specific health issues. In order to read these signs, you need to be in tune with your body and be observant enough to pick up on something that doesn't seem or feel right. Here are some examples:

- A feeling of constant stress or anxiety

- A lack of energy

- Chronic pain in your joints or other parts of your body

- Chronic fatigue

- Inability to perform daily activities easily

- Issues with one or more of your functional systems (e.g., problems with digestion)

- Frequent sickness

- Shortness of breath or difficulty in breathing

- Frequent headaches or migraines

Rational signs within the dimension of physical well-being, and physical signs may seem similar, but in actuality, have a couple of key differences.

1. **Data versus Feelings:** Rational signs around physical well-being are fact-based and indisputably tied to your physical health. For instance, you either do or do not have a BMI that indicates you are overweight or obese; you either do or do not exercise; you either do or do not have high blood pressure. Essentially, rational signs within the dimension of physical well-being can be seen via a test or an exam that would produce a positive or negative result, a yes or no answer. Physical signs, however, are less black and white, and show as symptoms rather than through data. They are dependent on physical feelings or sensations that we experience. For instance, you *feel* pain or *experience* stress.

2. **Constant versus Situational:** Unlike rational signs, which tend to be relatively constant regardless of circumstances, physical signs can either be constant throughout a multitude of circumstances or can be isolated to specific situations or environments. For instance, you may feel stress at your job, but the stress dissipates when you leave work and go home to family or friends.

Understanding the distinction between the two types of signs (rational signs pertaining to physical well-being versus physical signs) is important because it will help you identify in which dimensions you really need to focus. Whenever possible you will want to identify the environments or situations that cause physical signs to manifest themselves, as it will provide insight in understanding what kind of changes might be beneficial.

Since physical signs are often unpleasant or uncomfortable, they may be more motivating than rational signs. That being said, they may not fully tap into your emotional side, so may not be the best incentive to get you to want to make change in the end.

EMOTIONAL SIGNS

Emotional signs are the most motivating of the three types, and thus are probably the most important in helping us make change that sticks. They are, however, a bit more challenging to recognize.

First, in order to fully identify them, you must be comfortable acknowledging and understanding your emotions and feelings. If you tend to push feelings aside or are inclined to stifle them, it will be more difficult to pick up on emotional indicators. Second, emotional signs aren't always clear and can often be muddied by a variety of factors. If, for instance, you feel bad or guilty about feelings, your rational side may try to talk you out of your emotions or convince you that you are being overly sensitive. This clouds feelings, making them more difficult to read. Third, human emotions are very complex. And even though we may think we have the ability to understand what we are feeling, our emotions can be a result of many factors that make them far from clear-cut.

Since identifying our emotional signs can be a bit challenging, it may be helpful to categorize them via the six dimensions of well-being. The list of signs in the "Emotional Signs" chart below isn't exhaustive, but it should give you a sense for some of the typical feelings you might experience within each dimension.

EMOTIONAL SIGNS

Dimensions	Emotional Signs
Career	• You feel burned out. • You don't feel appreciated or respected at your job. • You dread going to work every day. • You aren't enthusiastic or passionate about the work you do.
Physical	• You find yourself using food as a source of happiness or comfort. • You lack self-control. • You aren't disciplined. • You don't like your body.
Social	• You feel unsure of your relationships. • Relationships leave you feeling bad about yourself or cause you to feel doubt. • Although friends and family physically surround you, you feel very lonely. • You don't trust or respect your friends or partner.
Emotional	• You feel chronically sad or down. • You feel negative toward most things in your life. • You feel overwhelmed by life's challenges. • You let your fears prevent you from experiencing all that life has to offer.
Intellectual	• You lack enthusiasm for interests or passions. • You are often bored, but aren't motivated in any way. • You feel that your life is one-dimensional (e.g., you spend all your time working). • You are indecisive or doubt the decisions you do make.
Spiritual	• You feel your life lacks purpose or direction. • You feel empty. • You don't feel at peace. • You have feelings of doubt, fear, disappointment, or despair.

PRIMARY VERSUS SECONDARY PHYSICAL SIGNS

How we feel mentally or emotionally can have a direct impact on how we feel physically. This is generally referred to as a *mind-body connection*. When we experience negative emotions, especially over a protracted period of time, this can result in physical symptoms much like the physical signs discussed on pages 40 and 41. In these circumstances, our physical signs are secondary and are a result of the situation we are in or a specific experience, and are not necessarily a reflection of our physical health.

For instance, if you are frustrated (emotional sign) at work because you are fighting internally with all your coworkers about a very important policy change, you may experience stress, fatigue, and chronic pain in your chest area (physical signs). If you were to remove the situation or trigger of work, however, the physical symptoms of stress, fatigue, and chronic pain may never show. In this case, the physical signs are a direct result of the situation, making them secondary. Although it might be beneficial to have your physical signs or symptoms looked at by a medical professional, there is a good chance that a change within the dimension of your career might be what is most needed.

On the other hand, if you find you are generally happy and feel fulfilled within all dimensions of well-being, but physical signs present themselves on a regular basis, it means the physical symptoms are primary and your physical well-being may be in jeopardy. As a result, you may seriously benefit from change within the dimension of physical well-being.

All three types of indicators—rational, physical, and emotional—are helpful in identifying areas for change. As mentioned, however, your emotional indicators will most likely motivate you for the longer term. If emotional signs are presenting themselves within a specific dimension of well-being, change may be warranted within that dimension. If, however, a dimension of well-being exhibits emotional indicators, as well as physical and/or rational indicators, you know you've hit on an area that would greatly benefit from change.

STEP 2: TAKE A HIGH-LEVEL ASSESSMENT

Although you might have a sense of the changes you'd like to make, it is good to get a high-level understanding of how you feel about each dimension of well-being.

Step 2 Tasks

Use the **Dimensions of Well-Being Self-Assessment** template in **Part III: The New You Journal** to assess how you feel about each of the dimensions of well-being today:

1. **Rate Importance:** In the column titled "Importance," rate each dimension of well-being on a scale of 1 to 10 (1 as the lowest and 10 as the highest) as to how important it is to you and your ability to be happy.

2. **Rate Satisfaction:** In the column titled "Satisfaction," rate each dimension on a scale of 1 to 10 (1 as extremely dissatisfied and 10 as extremely satisfied) in regard to how satisfied you are within each dimension today. If, for instance, you find all your relationships with family and friends rewarding and fulfilling, and you feel happy and content socially, you might rate the dimension of social well-being high. If, however, you find many of your relationships unsatisfactory or unrewarding, then you might rate it low.

3. **Identify Potential Dimensions for Change:** Circle the dimensions of well-being you rated highest in importance (over 5) and lowest in satisfaction. These are the dimensions you feel are most important yet are causing you the most discontent. These misalignments are likely contributing a great deal to your current dissatisfaction and are areas you may want to focus on as you continue on your path to personal reinvention.

Although this self-assessment may seem pretty rudimentary, it drives preliminary awareness around your feelings within each dimension. A heightened awareness will continue to be an important aspect of the process.

STEP 3: IDENTIFY THE SIGNS

Now that you have a good understanding of the different types of signs that can present themselves, it is time to identify the rational, physical, and emotional signs that may be showing within your own life. Regardless of the dimensions you identified in Step 2, look at all dimensions of well-being for this exercise. You may find there are areas you didn't think were causing unhappiness that are, or you may come to learn that the dimensions you thought you wanted to change were in actuality not the source of your current discontent.

> **Step 3 Tasks**
>
> Using the **Personal Signs of Change Matrix** template in **Part III: The New You Journal**, take a survey of each dimension of well-being. Think about what signs for change have manifested within each. You may find that you haven't experienced any signs in some of the dimensions or, for that matter, haven't experienced all three types—rational, physical, and emotional. Your job during this step, however, is to document as many of the signs you know to be present.
>
> 1. **Rational Signs:** Rational signs are the most obvious since they tend to be fact-based. For each dimension, identify any rational signs you feel are present. Document these in the column labeled "Rational Signs."
>
> 2. **Physical Signs:** Since we know that physical symptoms may or may not be tied to multiple dimensions of well-being, the column labeled "Physical Signs" spans across all dimensions. Later, you'll try to identify if they are primary or secondary indicators. Ask yourself the following:
>
> - Are there any physical signs I've been experiencing recently that may be of concern?
>
> - Have I been experiencing any discomfort, pain, or other physical symptoms?

3. **Emotional Signs:** Finally, for each dimension of well-being, document all the emotional signs you have been experiencing. Start by looking at some of the emotional-sign examples provided in **Step 1: Understand the Types of Signs** for some ideas. Do any of the signs resonate with you? Are any of them present in your life? To dig a bit deeper, ask yourself the following questions and document your answers in the column labeled "Emotional Signs":

- How do I feel about this dimension of well-being?

- Are there any negative emotions I've been experiencing?

- Do I feel any strong resentment, concerns, worry, or other issues within this dimension?

- Do I feel a strong desire to change something?

Take your time during Step 3. You may even want to think about your responses over a couple of days. And of course, be honest with yourself. There may be some dimensions in which you sincerely can't think of any signs, and that is OK. It probably means they are dimensions of well-being in which you are relatively content or have little concern.

> ## ROADBLOCK: COMPLACENCY
>
> *Complacency* means being satisfied yet unaware of actual problems, concerns, or deficiencies. In short, it signifies a false sense of contentment. If you are reading this book in the hopes of going through a personal reinvention and haven't uncovered signs that something needs to change, you may be in a state of complacency. If you think this is a roadblock you've hit, ask yourself the following questions:
>
> Why did I decide to read this book?
>
> What was my original motivation to change?
>
> What feelings or thoughts caused me to believe change was necessary?
>
> Am I repressing or afraid of my feelings?
>
> Has anything changed since I started reading this book?
>
> Although complacency can set in, you can definitely get yourself out of the rut. Remember that in Part I we discussed the "Aha! moment" of knowing something needs to change. Try to recapture that feeling. Remind yourself of when and where you felt it. Think about why you are unsatisfied and try to find a sense of urgency within yourself that prompts you to want to begin this process.

STEP 4: FEEL THE IMPACT

Now that you've identified all the various signs you've been experiencing, it's time to do some analysis to understand how much they are really impacting you. Obviously, we all experience negative or unfavorable emotions or symptoms at one time or another, but if they are fleeting, there may not be need for concern. It just may mean you are having a bad day or a bad week, or even a bad month. If, however, the signs are frequent or chronic, then you may have hit upon something important, and change is likely warranted.

Step 4 Tasks

Look at your **Personal Signs of Change Matrix** from **Step 3: Identify the Signs** and ask yourself the following questions:

1. How often do I experience these indicators? Do they occur rarely or often? Do they occur once a year? Once a month? Once a week? Every day?

2. How do I feel about this frequency? Does it feel overwhelming or is it manageable?

3. How much do I want to change this indicator? How would I feel if I could make it go away? Would I feel like a new person? Would I feel the same?

The questions above are meant to help you feel each sign's impact. The feeling behind the sign is what will drive you to want to change, not the sign itself. If the probing questions elicit a passionate emotional response, then the sign really is an indication that change is needed. If, however, you find you are answering these questions rather flatly, with very little emotion attached, it may not be impacting you that much.

4. Highlight the signs in the matrix that elicited a strong emotional response to the above questions. You can circle them, highlight them in yellow, or use whatever tool you want; just make them stand out.

The signs you've highlighted indicate that change is strongly needed. They are your Signs of Significance (SOS), and are your starting point for your personal reinvention.

ROADBLOCK: Emotional Disconnection

If you tend to disconnect from your emotions, you'll want to focus on becoming more in tune with them. It is important to connect to your emotions to understand how they influence your thoughts and behaviors. It is somewhat natural to want to avoid negative or unpleasant feelings, such as sadness, anger, or fear, yet these emotions are crucial to igniting the passion within to make change. Further, if you tend to stifle your negative emotions, it is highly possible that you do this with positive ones as well. Work on feeling and connecting with your emotions by doing the following:

Practice Empathy: If you find it difficult to express emotions about your own life, try doing it for others. You can either look toward friends or family who are going through an emotional experience and work at fully empathizing with them, or if you are uncomfortable with that, watch a movie or read a book that may be especially thought provoking or emotionally gripping. Imagine you are one of the characters who might be struggling emotionally with a situation. Try to feel her pain, her sadness, and even her joy. Use a section in your journal to describe how you might feel if you were in her situation.

Solicit Other People's Responses: Some people have difficulty acknowledging their emotions because they have never been allowed to, and so they shut them off. They grew up believing that feelings, especially those that were negative, were unacceptable. If you feel this describes your situation, look to other people you know who are good at expressing emotion, both good and bad. Talk to them about experiences they have found difficult. And if they have gone through similar experiences to yours, that might even be better. Identifying with others and their feelings may make it easier and more acceptable to express your own.

Pay Attention: Designate a space in your journal where you specifically focus on capturing feelings and emotions. Start paying more attention to your reactions and thoughts in a variety of situations. Ask yourself probing questions, especially when you sense an unpleasant reaction brimming. For instance, you might ask:

How would I describe the way I feel?

How is my body reacting to this situation?

Am I angry? Am I sad? Am I frustrated?

Why do I feel this way?

The more you practice getting in touch with your emotions, the easier it will become. Make a concerted effort to practice on a daily basis.

Putting energy into modifying behaviors or making change around those areas that you don't have much passion for may not be very long-lived. Think of it in this way: in **Step 3: Identify the Signs**, you identified what brings you discontent. In Step 4 you have now tried to identify the passion or feeling behind the discontent. When you put the two together, you have the first Principle of Change:

Principle of Change #1
DISCONTENT + PASSION DRIVE CHANGE.

STEP 5: ASSESS CAUSES OF RATIONAL AND EMOTIONAL SOS

With some signs it may be quite clear as to what is causing them, but with others you may have to do a little more investigation.

Step 5 Tasks

Using the **Rational and Emotional SOS Assessment** template in **Part III: The New You Journal**, list the rational and emotional signs you highlighted in **Step 4: Feel the Impact** (your physical signs will be addressed in the next step) under the column titled "Emotional Signs of Significance" for each dimension of well-being. For each SOS, ask yourself the following questions:

1. Why do I think these signs are presenting themselves?

2. What do I think the root causes of these signs are?

In the column labeled "Possible Cause," write what you believe to be is the cause of each SOS. Really think about it in detail and try to dig below the surface. Understanding what is causing your signs to show will help you to identify what needs to change. This will be instrumental to designing your vision in Stage 3 and creating a plan in Stage 4.

STEP 6: ASSESS CAUSES OF PHYSICAL SOS

As we discussed earlier, physical signs can be either primary or secondary. If they are secondary, it will be especially important to understand what might be causing them to appear. Physical signs can often result from several triggers or root causes. For instance, if you are feeling stressed, it might be a result of a stressful work environment, a stressful home life, and an inability to regularly get to the gym to release stress. Understanding all the triggers involved will help you to be more thorough in making change. If one of the causes isn't identified, and thus not addressed in your vision or plan, you may not see as much improvement in your happiness as if it was.

If you haven't identified any physical signs of significance, feel free to skip this step; otherwise, continue.

Step 6 Tasks

Using the **Physical SOS Assessment** template in **Part III: The New You Journal**, respond to the following:

In the column labeled "Physical Signs of Significance," list all the physical signs of significance you highlighted in **Step 4: Feel the Impact**.

1. In the column labeled "When SOS Occurs," answer the following:

• When do I generally experience this symptom or indicator?

- Is it during a specific scenario or within a specific environment?

- Or, do I feel this symptom at all times?

If you find that the symptom occurs often, it is highly possible that it is a direct result of a lack in physical well-being and is a primary physical sign. If, however, the symptom occurs only in certain situations, it means it is likely a secondary sign and may be tied to another dimension of well-being.

2. If physical signs occur only during certain situations, they are likely secondary. If so, you should be able to correlate them to a dimension of well-being (other than physical) that is likely the primary cause. In the column labeled "Possible Dimension of Well-Being," write in the dimension(s) to which you feel each sign is likely attributed.

KEY FACTORS FOR SUCCESS DURING STAGE 1

To successfully complete Stage 1, the following key factors for success will be important:

1. EMOTIONAL INTELLIGENCE

Emotional intelligence is crucial to this first stage and will continue to be important throughout the other five stages as well. It gives you the ability to recognize and assess your emotions and how they impact your thoughts and behavior. It also enables you to manage your feelings, even those that are hurtful or negative, in healthy and constructive ways so you can rationally approach change for a better future.

2. AN ABILITY TO TRUST YOUR INTUITION

Intuition is a "gut feeling" or a "sixth sense" about something. It is important in identifying signs as they present themselves, and assessing situations to understand what may be OK and what isn't. If you find it difficult to trust your own intuition, there are a few things you can do to develop the skill:

1. **Enjoy the Silence:** Give yourself time each day to meditate and focus in silence. Calm your mind by attempting not to think or analyze problems. Instead, be open and let your thoughts flow freely. Let your thoughts guide you instead of you guiding them.

2. **Be Alert:** Intuition is often built on what is going on around you. Observe your surroundings and environment, listen carefully to your thoughts and responses, and gather information accordingly.

3. **Go with Your Gut:** If something doesn't "feel right" then there is a good chance it isn't. Instead of arguing away those feelings, or coming up with reasons why you shouldn't think a certain way, listen to your inner voice. Practice trusting it and making decisions predicated on what your gut tells you.

The more you practice the above, the more you'll build confidence in your ability to listen to your intuition.

Stage 1 Summary

Stage 1 is focused on learning to identify the signs that change is needed, and mapping them to appropriate dimensions of well-being. The steps of Stage 1 are as follows:

Step 1: Understand the Types of Signs. A need for change manifests itself in one of three types of signs: rational, physical, or emotional.

Step 2: Take a High-Level Assessment. Assess the importance and satisfaction you feel within each dimension of well-being to gauge areas for change.

Step 3: Identify the Signs. Identify rational, physical, and emotional signs you have been experiencing within each dimension of well-being.

Step 4: Feel the Impact. Assess the impact of each sign to evaluate if it is a Sign of Significance (SOS).

Step 5: Assess Causes of Rational and Emotional SOS. Assess root causes of rational and emotional Signs of Significance.

Step 6: Assess Causes of Physical SOS: Assess root causes of physical Signs of Significance and to which dimensions of well-being they may be linked.

Principle of Change #1
DISCONTENT + PASSION DRIVE CHANGE.

STAGE 2: DISCOVER YOURSELF

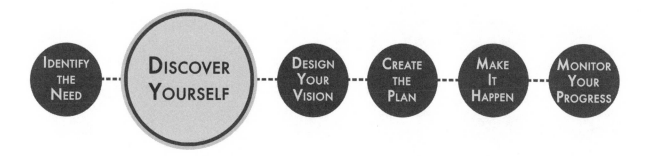

Knowing others is intelligence; knowing yourself is true wisdom.
Mastering others is strength; mastering yourself is true power.

—Tao Te Ching

To SUCCESSFULLY UNDERGO A PERSONAL REINVENTION and be your best, you need to have a deep understanding of yourself: how you've become the person you are today, and where your perspectives and thoughts originated. In short, you want to uncover your authentic self.

The self-discovery process is probably the most intense yet rewarding stage of the process. It is likely that you will spend a bit of time going through this stage. Through a variety of self-assessments and activities, you'll uncover and gain further insight into your values, talents, passions, upbringing, and social and environmental influences, as well as the life experiences that have made you who you are and influence how you think and behave. Essentially, you are building self-awareness.

When we have a strong sense of self-awareness, we are able to take responsibility for our thoughts, decisions, and actions. When we don't, we can easily be influenced by other people, making decisions that are predicated on their interests, belief systems, and desires and not our own. Self-awareness also enables us to create our own dreams so that we can live the life we want as opposed to living out dreams that have been handed down to us or put upon us by family members, friends, colleagues, and other individuals who may have agendas separate from ours.

In *The 7 Habits of Highly Effective People*, Stephen Covey explains that there are three root causes that determine how we respond to situations and to life circumstances. The first, *genetic determinism*, implies that your responses are based on genetics: you are predisposed to act or think a certain way because you genetically inherited these tendencies. The second, *psychic determinism*, is based on the principle that your upbringing and childhood experiences have influenced your responses and character. And the third, *environmental determinism*, suggests that someone or something in your environment influences your responses. All three have merit, so all three will be addressed in the pages that follow.

Self-discovery and building self-awareness are paramount to your ability to change and successfully undergo personal reinvention. They lay the foundation and groundwork for you to move forward through the next four stages of the path in a way that is most effective to you personally. This is essentially the second Principle of Change.

Principle of Change #2
SELF-AWARENESS IS THE FOUNDATION FOR CHANGE.

DID YOU KNOW? SELF-AWARENESS AND ITS IMPACT ON OUR RELATIONSHIPS

Not only does building self-awareness benefit ourselves, but it can also help us in relating to others and building healthy, sound relationships. When we are self-aware, it makes us more capable of being honest with ourselves about our own flaws, which in turn makes it easier to be honest with others. This makes us more likable. Further, self-awareness gives us the ability to be open, thoughtful, and aware of how we impact others. This promotes empathy, tolerance, and humility.

STAGE 2 ACTION STEPS

Activities within **Stage 2: Discover Yourself** involve tremendous introspection, and a lot of mental and emotional energy. This stage should not be rushed. If you haven't fully read through all of Part II as recommended earlier in the book, I suggest that you at least consider a read-through of all of Stage 2 before attempting any of the exercises on the following pages. This will give you time to fully grasp the questions asked so you can be thoughtful in your responses.

Each activity should be done slowly. With some activities you may even consider taking a day before responding so you have time to process your thoughts before completing the step. This will help encourage accuracy and authenticity.

ROADBLOCK: OTHER PEOPLE'S OPINIONS AND INPUT

We can often fall victim to relying on what other people think to help guide us in developing a perspective or viewpoint, or even to see the reality of a situation. Although this can be helpful, it can throw us off course when we are trying to recognize and listen to our own thoughts and feelings. If an individual providing his opinion or perspective doesn't understand you and what you need or value, he could be giving you misguided information or insight. Further, if he is coming from a psychologically unhealthy place, he may have a distorted perspective.

Instead of relying on the opinions of others to give you insight during self-discovery and other parts of the process, try to focus on your own thoughts, feelings, memories, and experiences as much as possible. Begin setting boundaries with individuals who tend to give their unsolicited "two cents." Let them know that although you appreciate their thoughts, opinions, and concern, you need to listen more to your own thoughts and emotions. If they care for you, they will respect your wishes.

STEP 1: DEFINE YOUR VALUES

Your values are what make up your core beliefs and are the driving force behind everything you think and do, who you are, and what you stand for. They are a result of your experiences and influences throughout your lifetime, including your upbringing, education, religious affiliation, friends and family, and more. They are instrumental to helping you make decisions that are in your best interest and guiding you in creating the life you want.

Your values run deep and are fairly stable in nature. They provide a foundation from which to solve problems, maximize opportunities, and continually grow. That said, how your values are realized can differ depending on where you are in your life.

> *Throughout Kimberly's life, success was one of her core values. During adolescence and young adulthood, success was tied very closely to her achievement in school and business. When she was a high school student, success meant earning straight A's in all her classes. When she graduated high school, success meant getting into the number one college of her choice. And, when she graduated college, the type of job she was able to secure and the salary she earned was what represented success. Even when she married her husband, Evan, the money she made and the position she held at her company was how she defined success.*

> *When Kimberly was thirty-four, however, she and her husband had their first child, Emily. When Emily was born, Kimberly's view of success began to take on a whole new meaning. Although she still valued earning good money, she realized that the time she spent with her daughter was more valuable. As a result, Kimberly redefined success as effectively balancing work, life, and her family, as well as being a good mom.*

As you can see, success was a core value for Kimberly and remained so throughout various stages of her life. How she defined success, however, changed. When she was young, success was defined by her achievements in school and at work. When she became a parent, however, success was defined by a different set of criteria, including family, a work-life balance, and being a good parent.

A solid understanding of your values will enable you to maintain a strong center core from which to live your life. Your values require no justification to others and will enable you to make optimal decisions. In order to successfully make change, it will be important to adhere to your values as you design your vision for the future in Stage 3 and create the plan to achieve it in Stage 4. Doing so ensures you stay true to yourself. The more your vision and plan are in alignment with your values, the more you will continue to feel inspired and invigorated to forge ahead with the changes you want to make.

Step 1 Tasks

Using the **My Values Worksheet** in **Part III: The New You Journal** as a template, document your responses to the following tasks:

1. Ask yourself, "What is important to me?" Don't think too much about this question. In the column labeled "Values," write down all the words that come to mind without censoring anything. Avoid listing anything you feel you *should* write down and instead, focus on what truly speaks to you at a deeper level. Also, try to keep your responses to one-word answers and avoid lengthy phrases or sentences.

2. If you really struggled with the first task, or you feel like you need some inspiration, look at the "List of Values" chart below, and add any words that strongly resonate with you to your list from Task 1.

3. Assess each value on your list and provide one of the following ratings in the column labeled "Rating": *A* for extremely important, *B* for moderately important, or *C* for not that important. Attempt to have no more than five to ten values rated as an *A*. If you notice that some of the values you've selected are similar, try combining them so there aren't any duplicates or overlapping values on your list. Some examples of similar or overlapping values are: determination and perseverance; candor and honesty; kindness and compassion.

4. Using the **My Most Important Values Worksheet** in **Part III: The New You Journal** as a template, list the values you marked with an *A* in the column labeled "My Most Important Values." Go through all the values and rank each of the five to ten values in order of importance in the column labeled "Ranking" (1 would be most important, and 10 would be the least important).

5. The top five values ranked in your list are your core values. Write these five values under the "Core Values" heading on the worksheet.

Once you've chosen your core values, you can apply them to the work you do throughout your path to personal reinvention. These values should also be your guide through life, through work, and at home. They will enable you to create the life you want.

List of Values

Acceptance	Compassion	Fame	Ingenuity	Selflessness
Achievement	Confidence	Family	Insightfulness	Sensitivity
Adaptability	Conformity	Fearlessness	Integrity	Serenity
Adventure	Consistency	Fidelity	Intelligence	Service
Affection	Contentment	Financial	Kindness	Sexuality
Affluence	Control	Independence	Knowledge	Simplicity
Agility	Conviction	Fitness	Leadership	Solitude
Ambition	Courage	Flexibility	Learning	Spirituality
Appreciation	Creativity	Flow	Love	Stability
Authenticity	Credibility	Focus	Making a	Strength
Balance	Curiosity	Forgiveness	Difference	Structure
Beauty	Decisiveness	Frankness	Modesty	Success
Being the Best	Dependability	Freedom	Nurturing	Sympathy
Belonging	Determination	Friends	Openness	Teamwork
Bravery	Devotion	Gratitude	Organization	Temperance
Brilliance	Devoutness	Growth	Passion	Thankfulness
Calmness	Dignity	Happiness	Peace	Thoroughness
Candor	Diligence	Hard Work	Perseverance	Timeliness
Care	Discipline	Health	Playfulness	Trust
Career	Diversity	Helpfulness	Poise	Unity
Challenge	Effectiveness	Honesty	Polish	Valor
Charity	Elegance	Honor	Power	Vigor
Cheerfulness	Empathy	Hopefulness	Prosperity	Virtue
Clear-	Energy	Humor	Quality	Vision
Mindedness	Enthusiasm	Hygiene	Resolve	Willpower
Cleverness	Enterprise	Impact	Respect	Wisdom
Closeness	Excellence	Inner	Self-	Wit
Comfort	Expertise	Harmony	Actualization	Youthfulness
Commitment	Faith	Innovation	Self-Control	Zeal

THE BENEFITS OF HAVING A STRONG SENSE OF VALUES

- Goal Setting: Following a life predicated on your values gives you direction in setting your goals. This enables you to set goals true to what is important to you and not what is important to others.

- Better Decision Making: Your values give you a foundation from which to make all decisions. They ensure that your actions are in alignment with what you find important. Without a solid understanding of your values, it is easy to base decisions on circumstances and social pressures instead of on what you value.

- Happiness: When we are clear on our values, and make choices in alignment with them, we promote happiness. When we don't, we can experience internal conflict, which ultimately leads to unhappiness.

- Self-Confidence: Staying true to your values helps build self-confidence. You feel surer of your choices, the decisions you make, your character, and who you are. Further, your behaviors are more consistent and authentic.

STEP 2: IDENTIFY YOUR STRENGTHS AND ACKNOWLEDGE YOUR WEAKNESSES

Each individual comes with an innate set of strengths and a set of weaknesses. Strengths are those things that you do well, seemingly effortlessly. They come very naturally to you and aren't a result of acquired knowledge or skill but instead are a result of your natural abilities.

According to Marcus Buckingham and Donald O. Clifton in *Now, Discover Your Strengths*, we devote more time to fixing our shortcomings than to developing our strengths. Focusing on our weaknesses doesn't allow us to fully maximize our talents, however, and can have a significant impact on our ability to be successful. Buckingham and Clifton's research shows that individuals who do not capitalize on their strengths at work tend to dread going to work, have more negative interactions and feelings about their company, are less inclined to have creative moments, are less productive, and treat customers poorly. Those who work from a place of strength, however, are much more productive, are more engaged, and feel they have an excellent quality of life. Although most of their research applies to work and career, these same principles can be applied to life as a whole. The more we tap into our talents and strengths, the more we will feel fulfilled and find happiness and success in all areas of life.

Tony was very out of shape and knew that he needed to lose weight. Unfortunately, due to his short attention span and competitive spirit, he was never very good at doing the same exercises over and over again (running, walking, weight training) with no obvious goal or "win" attached. As such, he struggled with going to the gym. He even found working with some of the best trainers to be rather boring. As a result, his multiple attempts at joining gyms and working with trainers failed miserably. Losing weight continued to be a struggle.

In exploring his strengths, Tony was reminded of his days in high school and college, when he played team sports and was particularly talented at tennis. He thrived on the competition of the game, and it came very easily to him. Although it had been some time (about fifteen years) since he had played, the idea of doing something he was good at seemed rather appealing and inspired him to take up the sport again. Even though a lot of time had passed, he hoped his talent might make up for his lack of athleticism, at least in the short term.

Tony joined a tennis club and started to play regularly, and as he suspected, his talent and strength in the game compensated for his lack in physical fitness. This kept him motivated to continue playing. He eventually lost the thirty pounds he had gained over the last five years. Tony felt great physically and mentally, and as a result, started enjoying other activities as well.

By tapping into his strengths, Tony was motivated to make the change he desired. Yet when he attempted to approach the change from a place of weakness and disinterest, he failed. Capitalizing on your strengths will not only build self-confidence but will also keep you motivated for the longer term.

Step 2 requires that you recognize those things you do best. What are your talents? What can you do better than most other people? Identifying your strengths should be very automatic. You can also ask others who know you well to do this exercise with you too. People who are close to you may have helpful feedback, but remember: in the end, you know yourself the best.

Step 2 Tasks

My Strengths

Using the **My Strengths Worksheet** in **Part III: The New You Journal** as your template, complete the following tasks:

1. In the column titled "Strengths," write down a list of your strengths and talents within each dimension of well-being. Try not to confuse your strengths and talents with knowledge or skill. Instead, focus on those activities or traits that come to you easily and naturally. To help you with the process, answer the following four questions:

    •   What am I good at that doesn't require very much effort?

    •   What do I do better than most other people?

    •   When do I feel like I'm in a "zone" of productivity, accomplishment, success, and happiness all at once?

    •   What do other people tell me I'm excellent at doing?

2. Narrow down the list to no more than three strengths within each dimension of well-being. Ideally, you want to highlight those strengths that:

    •   Are your strongest

    •   You can show several examples for, exhibiting why they are your strengths

    •   You enjoy using or working with

3. For each strength you choose, write down a story that demonstrates how it is one of your strengths in the column labeled "Examples."

My Weaknesses

Now it is time to think about your weaknesses. Although your vision and plan should capitalize on your strengths, it will be helpful to understand what activities or things cause you the most frustration or require the most effort. This will help you to avoid developing a plan that will require extensive use of your weaknesses, which could cause wasted time and energy. Using the **My Weaknesses Worksheet** in **Part III: The New You Journal** as a template, complete the following tasks for each dimension of well-being:

1.   In the column labeled "Weaknesses to Avoid," provide a list of what you think you struggle with the most for each dimension of well-being. To help, answer the following questions:

•   What am I not good at?

•   What activities do I least enjoy?

•   What frustrates me the most?

2.   Narrow the list down to three weaknesses per dimension. Reliance on these weaknesses should be avoided or minimized as you design your vision and create a plan for your personal reinvention.

STEP 3: IDENTIFY AND ADDRESS YOUR FEARS

All of us have experienced fear, anxiety, or stress at some point. Unfortunately, the more we experience these emotions, the less we feel comfortable taking risks, managing change, and moving forward with our goals. The more energy we spend in avoiding what we fear, the less energy we have to actively pursue what we want. Many of us let our fear of the unknown impair our ability to be positive, to plan for the future, or to achieve the things that will bring us the most happiness.

Although fear is a very real feeling, it is often not based in reality. Fear stems from what we imagine to be possible when we move out of our comfort zone and into the unknown. It is rarely based on fact. We tend to imagine the worst-case scenario instead of the best, and this propels us into a state of anxiety.

John worked for his company for over twenty years, yet he was very unhappy. He was working with people who he felt didn't respect him or value his talents, and he knew he was drastically underpaid. Further, he knew that he was capable of working in a position at a higher level. Yet John struggled to look for a new job because he was doubtful that he would find what he was looking for, and worse, he feared rejection.

While looking online for job openings within his industry, John found the perfect position...a dream job. John's experience made him an ideal candidate. Further, the pay was better and the work was a better match for his talents and skills. When he started the application process, he was overcome by fear of rejection. His fear consumed him to such an extent that he convinced himself that he didn't really want the position, making up numerous reasons as to why it was not a good match. But most of them were based in fear, not reality. His excuses included:

1. *His commute would be too long. The reality: it was an extra ten minutes.*
2. *He thought it would be difficult to take time off for the interviews. The reality: he had an extra five days of paid time off (PTO) he hadn't used from the prior year and all of his PTO from the current year. Moreover, he wasn't heavily supervised, giving him flexibility to leave his office throughout the day.*
3. *He thought he should be thankful for the job he had in an economic downturn. The reality: companies were hiring again.*
4. *He believed he wasn't really qualified. The reality: he was overqualified for the job he presently had and perfectly qualified for the job under consideration.*
5. *He worried that the new job in question could be worse than his current job. The reality: his current job was making him miserable. He really had nothing to lose.*

John never applied for the job. His fears limited him from taking the risk to make the change he so desperately wanted. His colleague Tim, however, did. Tim was junior to John, and wasn't as qualified or skilled. Even so, Tim ended up getting the position. When John found out, he was frustrated and filled with resentment.

John missed out on an opportunity to improve the quality of his life and his career. His fears limited his ability to make change, and instead he stayed in the same unfulfilling job, unhappy and stagnant. What is worse, he became bitter and resentful, because he knew deep down that someone less qualified got the job he really wanted. These negative feelings only compounded to make him unhappier.

Fear is debilitating. It cripples us and doesn't allow us to take necessary risks when we need to. Instead, we spend our time looking for the "safe way" of doing things, which can limit our ability to experience anything at all. As a result, we miss out on what life has to offer. The best way to avoid limiting your life as a result of fear is to recognize your personal fears and confront them.

Step 3 Tasks

My Past Fears

Understanding past situations when you were fearful can be easier than addressing current fears. Over time, the fear subsides and we tend to gain perspective that allows us to see things a bit more clearly. Using the **My Past Fears Worksheet** in **Part III: The New You Journal** as a template, do for the following tasks:

1. Think back to the times you've been most fearful and were afraid to take action. Specifically focus on the fears that limited you. Write them in the column labeled "Past Fears."

2. Assess the emotions that were prevalent (and still may be) by providing responses to the following under the column labeled "Emotions":

- What emotions did I feel during these times?

- What was I most afraid of?

3. Assess the reality of the fears you experienced. Ask yourself the following questions and put your responses in the column labeled "Reality":

- Were my fears based on realistic concerns, or were they irrational?

- Is it possible that I made what I was fearful about scarier than it actually was?

- Were my fears based on past experiences or the actual situation?

4. Assess your ability to have controlled the situation you feared. If you had no control over it then your actions would have had no influence. In these situations, our fear isn't helpful; once again, it is debilitating. If, however, you did have control over the situation, provide answers to the following questions in the column labeled "Control":

- What could I have done to better control the situation?

- Was there anything I could have done to eliminate my fear?

5. For those fears that seemed to be the strongest, rewrite your stories in the section titled "A New Story of an Old Fear." Your stories should describe the best-case scenarios that could have occurred if you had confronted the fears and taken action. Discuss each fear, how you could have conquered it, and the positive outcomes that could have resulted.

My Current Fears

Now that you understand how fear has limited you in the past, you can learn from those experiences for the future. Looking back to the fears you described above, you will want to assess which fears still plague you today and what else you are afraid of. Use the **My Current Fears Worksheet** in **Part III: The New You Journal** as a template in responding to the following tasks:

1. In the column labeled "Current Fears," write in the fears from the past that you believe are still limiting you today. If you feel that you have new fears that you didn't have in the past, feel free to add those to the list as well.

2. In the column labeled "Control," assess if you have any control over your fears. Ask yourself:

- Do I have any control over the situations of which I'm fearful?

- Is there any way I can control my fear?

3. In the column labeled "What I Can Do," write down what you believe you can actively do to address the situation that is causing the fear.

4. Just as you did with your past fears, write a story that describes a best-case scenario of what would happen if you were to take the risk and push your fear aside. What would happen? What would the outcomes be? How would you feel? Write the story under the section titled "A Story of a Forgotten Fear."

Fears I've Conquered

Finally, there is a chance that you have had fears in the past that you actually conquered. If so, you are fortunate in that you can use those experiences to inspire and motivate you to address any current fears with which you are struggling. Respond to the following using the **My Conquered Fears Worksheet** in **Part III: The New You Journal** as a template:

1. In the column labeled "Conquered Fears," describe the fear you had.

2. In the column labeled "Cause," describe what caused you to feel the fear you felt.

3. In the column labeled "What I Did," describe what you did to overcome the fear.

4. In the column labeled "Outcome," describe how you felt after conquering the fear. Did you feel proud of yourself? Were you happy? Were you glad you took action?

5. For each fear you've conquered, summarize your story under the section titled "A Story of a Conquered Fear." This will be useful in the future when you find yourself feeling fearful. You can use these stories as reminders of how you were able to overcome your fears and the positive outcomes that resulted.

This step may have seemed long and tedious, but there is a lot of benefit to really understanding and getting to the heart of your fears. Doing so will help you address the fears and anxieties you have that debilitate you, preventing you from achieving goals, making change, and being your best.

As you continue to work on reinventing yourself, use this exercise as a reminder of how unrealistic fears often are and how you can overcome them. Remind yourself of the positive scenarios that can play out instead of dwelling on the negative. Push fear of the unknown out of your mind and be open to the possibilities instead. Reread your stories as you continue throughout your journey so you are continually inspired to overcome fear throughout the process.

STEP 4: IDENTIFY YOUR PASSIONS

Your passions are what drives you and what makes life worth living. They are the things that bring you joy and happiness. They are the things you do out of love, not out of guilt. They are what you are naturally predisposed to do, regardless of money or recognition.

When going through a personal reinvention, integrating your passions into the plan or action steps you develop will keep you engaged throughout the process.

Both of Joy's parents died when they were in their sixties from preventable diseases. Her grandparents, however, lived long, healthy lives. At the age of forty-seven, Joy had gained about forty pounds in one year. She realized that she was quickly following in her parents' footsteps, and wanted to reinvent herself to follow those of her grandparents instead.

As a librarian, Joy had a passion for reading. As a result, she decided to utilize her passion as a motivator to lose weight. She set a goal of reading one book for every pound she wanted to lose.

Books proved to be excellent guides, cheerleaders, and companions for Joy's weight-loss journey. Through reading, she was provoked to create a plan and stick to it. The tips and tricks she learned throughout the pages of all the books constantly encouraged her, even when failure seemed imminent. And, Joy's path seemed easier as a result of the many examples of dieters who made the journey before her and lived to write the tale.

Since creating her goal, Joy was able to lose over seventy pounds and read fifty-eight healthy-lifestyle books. Joy successfully reinvented her health. She went from overeating to careful eating, from obesity to normal weight, and from feeling pain in movement to grace and strength.

By tapping into her passion for reading, Joy's personal reinvention was much more enjoyable. She remained inspired and was successful in reaching her goals.

Step 4 Tasks

Using the **My Passions Worksheet** in **Part III: The New You Journal** as a template, do the following tasks:

1. Write a list of all the things you believe to be your passions in the column labeled "Passion." To help, you might want to ask yourself:

    •   What am I happiest doing?

    •   How would I most like to fill my time?

    •   What can I do for countless hours and never get bored?

2. In the column "How It Makes Me Feel," provide three adjectives that describe how you feel when you are tapping into each passion.

3. Provide examples of activities that may allow you to tap into your passions in the column labeled "How Can I Tap into This?" If you don't have any clear ideas about this now, don't worry; you'll have opportunities later in the process during **Stage 4: Create the Plan** to understand how your passions may play a part of your reinvention.

STEP 5: CELEBRATE YOUR ACCOMPLISHMENTS

Many of us find it difficult to acknowledge and celebrate our accomplishments. Yet documenting them and referring back to them regularly can provide inspiration for reaching future goals. Recognizing your accomplishments from the past instills confidence in taking on new challenges today and in the future. It also helps in overcoming fear when it rears its ugly head.

Step 5 Tasks

Use the **My Accomplishments Worksheet** in **Part III: The New You Journal** as a template in conducting the following tasks:

1. Think back to the times you accomplished things that were important to you. Write down each achievement in the column labeled "Accomplishment."

2. Take a minute to identify the emotions you felt as a result of your achievements. Write your emotions down under the column titled "The Way I Felt."

3. Think about how long it took for you to achieve what you did, and document it under the column "The Time It Took."

4. Take some time to remember the struggles, the ups and downs, the setbacks, the obstacles, and all you went through in order to reach your goal and accomplish what you set out to do. In the column titled "The Steps I Took," write down all the steps you took to overcome obstacles and to achieve what you did.

5. Look back at all you've documented. Try to summarize in one or two sentences the biggest lessons you learned from your achievements in the section titled "Lessons Learned."

STEP 6: LEARN FROM YOUR FAILURES

Although it may not seem like it, failure can be highly instrumental to your ability to succeed.

When we fail, we learn valuable lessons that provide us with insights and experience so that we can avoid making the same mistakes—or worse, bigger mistakes—down the line. When we fail and can recover, we learn to fear failure less and can see that risk taking isn't so scary. You become less sensitive to the impact of failing so that if it happens, the fall doesn't feel as hard. This makes it easier to get back up and try again. Finally, failure teaches us what works and what doesn't, ultimately increasing our chances of success down the line.

> That which does not kill us makes us stronger.
>
> *—Friedrich Nietzsche*

Tamara chose to end her seventeen-year marriage on the eve of her thirty-ninth birthday. After years of feeling unhappy and unfulfilled, Tamara had lost her self-esteem, confidence, and self-worth. The decision was extremely difficult, yet she saw the ending of her marriage as her only solution.

Leaving her marriage with three children, no career, and very little in the way of financial help, Tamara needed to find a job...fast. Having spent years as a stay-at-home mom, Tamara was confronted with the realization that she was not qualified or experienced to work at a job that would pay her enough to sufficiently support her children, and so she pursued her passion for fitness.

Tamara made the difficult decision to go away to school for eight weeks to become a licensed fitness professional. Leaving her children for that time not only caused her great guilt and emotional turmoil, but her friends and family criticized her as well. The lack of support caused her to doubt her decision and her dream of being who she wanted to be. When she returned from school, however, Tamara quickly began her career in personal training, and shortly thereafter was successful enough to open her own fitness company.

Today, Tamara is happy and is constantly excited about her future. She took what most people would see as failure and used it to create a life that she loves. Using her experience as an example, she inspires others to take risks and pursue a better life for themselves. Maybe the biggest benefit is how it has impacted her as a mother. Her children see their mom as a role model. They are proud of her and continue to share a rewarding, close relationship with her, more than they did before her transformation.

Tamara realized that by accepting the failure of her marriage, she was admitting that she was living a life that was inauthentic to who she was as a person. Letting go allowed her to become a more successful mother, business-woman, and person as a whole. She would not have had the courage to re-create herself without first hitting rock bottom.

Step 6 Tasks

Use the **My Failures Worksheet** in **Part III: The New You Journal** as a template while going through the following activities:

1. In the column labeled "Failures," write down what you perceive to be your top three biggest failures.

2. For each failure, write down three lessons you learned from the experience in the column labeled "Lessons Learned."

3. In the column labeled "Positive Impact," write down how each lesson learned has had a positive impact on your life or how it has led to unexpected success.

By doing this exercise, it should become clear that failure brings with it positive benefits, and it can act as a tool to help you achieve future success. As you continue through your process, capitalize on the lessons you've learned and the positive things that have come from perceived past failures.

STEP 7: DETERMINE YOUR MOTIVATORS

Motivators are what make us "tick." They drive us to succeed and to accomplish, and are at the very heart of personal and professional fulfillment. They influence our emotional side and are powerful tools in getting us to consistently move forward until we've succeeded, even after we experience failure. Our motivators inspire us and give us the incentive, the energy, and the passion to stay on course with whatever we set our minds to do.

Although your motivators may seem similar to your values, their roles are different. A value is the *what* of your core beliefs and center, while a motivator is the *why*—why your value is important to you. This relationship is further explained below via the "Values and Motivators" chart.

VALUES AND MOTIVATORS

Value (What)	Driver (Why)
Achievement	You feel good and proud of yourself when you successfully accomplish something.
Family	They provide a deep source of love, support, and happiness.
Power	You enjoy influencing others and feeling in control.

Your personal motivators are instrumental to staying engaged as you continue through the process of personal reinvention. Different things motivate each of us, and so it will be important to fine-tune your vision and plan to appeal to the motivators that personally drive you as an individual.

Step 7 Tasks

Use the **My Motivators Worksheet** in **Part III: The New You Journal** as a template to conduct the following tasks:

1. List the core values you uncovered in **Step 1: Define Your Values** under the column "Core Values."

2. For each core value, write down at least three reasons they are important to you in the column labeled "Motivators."

ROADBLOCK: An Inability to Let Go of Past Hurt

The self-discovery process may cause great and unexpected pain or hurt. If you find it difficult to move beyond the pain and resentment you unearth from your past experiences, practice the following:

1. **Feel It:** First, allow yourself to feel the hurt. Really feel it. Have a good cry if you want. You have every right to feel the emotions you do, and allowing yourself to feel pain from the past is an important first step toward moving forward.

2. **Analyze:** Once you've allowed yourself to grieve the past, switch into a more objective mode. Let your rational side identify what has caused the pain. Analyzing what is causing the pain allows you to address it. Ask yourself, "What might make the pain better?" If the pain is a result of another person or several people, maybe it would be helpful to discuss your feelings with those involved. In some cases, they may not even realize they hurt you. If so, they may actually want to know how you feel. The honest communication might ultimately strengthen your relationship.

3. **Forgive:** Next, practice forgiveness. Whether or not you are able to fully confront the cause of your pain, forgiveness will help you move on. Remind yourself that all of us are human and have our faults.

4. **Let Go:** Finally, let go. The past is the past. Learn from it. It is now time to create a new and better future. There will always be circumstances and people you can't change. Worrying about things you have no power over, however, will only cause more stress and negativity. Whenever you feel yourself focusing on the past, ask yourself if it's worth spending so much energy on something you can't change.

It will be important to factor in your motivators when designing your vision and creating your plan for change and personal reinvention. Doing so will help you accomplish more, achieve your goals, and ultimately find happiness.

STEP 8: UNDERSTAND YOUR UPBRINGING

Our upbringing has a tremendous impact on who we are, how we behave, and how we think. Our relationships with parents and siblings, our position within the family structure, and our experiences growing up all play a huge role in the development of our value system, our priorities and our personality, and how we function from day to day. Therefore, considering your family dynamic and your role within your family is instrumental to effectively creating a vision and plan for change.

Step 8 Tasks

Use the **My Upbringing Worksheet** in **Part III: The New You Journal** as a template to document your responses to the following questions:

1. On a scale of 1 to 10, how would you rate your overall happiness level in regard to your home life when you were a child (1 being not happy and 10 being extremely happy)?

2. Describe your family structure. Did you grow up with both a mom and a dad in your home? Did they stay married throughout your childhood? Do you have siblings? If so, what was your birth order? Describe your feelings about your family structure.

3. Answer the following questions for each family member you lived with:

   - What were their positive attributes, and how did they impact you?

   - What were their negative attributes, and how did they impact you?

   - How close were you?

   - How did you feel about your relationship with them?

4. In regard to your home life, how did you feel as a child? As a teenager? As a young adult? How do you feel today?

5. What did you like most about your upbringing?

6. What did you like least about your upbringing?

7. Looking back, do you feel there was anything lacking, or do you wish you could change any aspects of your upbringing? If so, what?

The point of this exercise is to uncover how much your upbringing has impacted your values, viewpoints, and behaviors. You may begin to see how your family and home life have influenced you and your outlook on life. You may start to see a correlation between your upbringing and your fears, past decisions, and even your personality. These insights can help guide you as you make changes, and help you fully understand when thoughts and behaviors are truly your own versus those that might have been due to familial experiences and influences.

STEP 9: EVALUATE OTHER LIFE EXPERIENCES

Similar to our family and upbringing, our experiences outside the home can have a tremendous impact on us. Both positive and negative experiences can cause us to look at life in certain ways, and possibly have fears or anxieties that might not have developed had those experiences not taken place. Many of the questions we ask in Step 9 are similar to those in Step 8.

Step 9 Tasks

Using the **My Life Experiences Worksheet** in **Part III: The New You Journal** as a template, document your responses to the following questions:

1. Outside of the home, describe how you felt as a child. How did you feel as a teenager? As a young adult?

2. Did you enjoy your experience in grade school? In high school? In college?

3. What kind of extracurricular activities were you involved with? Did you enjoy them? Describe your feelings about them and your interactions with other students or people involved.

4. How do you think the experiences from questions 2 and 3 have shaped you as a person?

5. How would you describe work experiences? How have you related to people you worked with? The work itself? The company?

6. List the five life experiences that provided you with the greatest level of pleasure and happiness. Describe in detail why they were so positive.

7. List the five life experiences that caused you pain or hurt, or provided you with the lowest level of pleasure or happiness. Describe in detail why these experiences were so negative. How have they impacted you today?

You may find there is quite a bit of overlap between your upbringing and your life experiences outside the home. What you experienced in school, extracurricular activities, and even on the playground may have required the involvement of parents or other family members.

For instance, let's say Allison is a third grader and is subjected to bullying in the classroom. Although the bullying is clearly a school-related experience, the way her family responds to the situation, if at all, could have a direct impact on her as well. The following scenarios are only a few of the countless ways her parents might handle the situation when Allison goes home and tells them about the bullying. Additionally, Allison's responses could vary within each scenario.

- **Scenario 1:** Her parents are dismissive or downplay the pain or hurt. One way this could impact Allison is that she could feel alone and invalidated. This could cause her to grow up doubting her emotions or shutting off her emotions altogether.

- **Scenario 2:** Her parents listen, are supportive, and validate her feelings. Allison might grow up to be well adjusted and comfortable with her emotions.

- **Scenario 3:** Her parents take action, calling the school to set up a meeting with the teacher, the bully, and the parents of the bully. Allison might feel loved, taken care of, secure, and protected.

- **Scenario 4:** Her parents become overprotective and overreactive. They pull Allison from the school and place her in a different school. This might cause Allison to grow up feeling uncomfortable with conflict, and she may struggle with feeling confident in handling difficult situations.

Obviously, there are an infinite number of ways this situation could play out, but each can have a profound impact on a child and the person she grows up to be. Even from child to child the results may differ, depending on the family dynamic, the child, and the additional experiences the child has growing up. The point is, however, that experiences both at home and outside the home impact us in how we behave, think, and act.

My Combined Experiences

Using the **My Combined Experiences Worksheet** in **Part III: The New You Journal** as a template, respond to the following questions:

1. What experiences at school or during extracurricular activities required the involvement of your parents or siblings?

2. How did they behave toward you? Toward the situation? Toward the other individuals involved?

3. How did you feel about the way they handled the situation?

4. Has any of this shaped who you are today?

Understanding these experiences may help you identify any lingering hurt or resentment you harbor as a result of situations or issues you've encountered in the past. Awareness of these feelings and how they impact you should be considered as you progress through the rest of the process.

STEP 10: DETERMINE WHAT YOU WANT

Now you will answer one of the most important questions of the self-discovery process: "What do you want?" In Stephen R. Covey's *The 7 Habits of Highly Effective People*, his second habit is "Begin with the end in mind." Practicing this helps us to think about what we want out of life without the limitations of our current situation. It takes us into the future, allowing us to think about what we hope our lives will have encompassed from a deeper place, as opposed to a superficial or materialistic viewpoint. Step 10 is a perfect time to implement this thought process.

Take some time and really think about this question and do so independently of everything and everyone else. Only you have the answer. The self-awareness you've developed through the previous nine steps should help you to avoid answering this question through fear, resentment, or anger. Also, avoid basing answers on a need for approval, or on proving yourself to the world. Instead, reach deep within and think about what *you* want out of life.

Step 10 Tasks

Using the **What I Want Worksheet** in **Part III: The New You Journal** as a template, imagine change is easy for just a minute, and answer the following questions as openly and honestly as possible.

1. When I look back on my life when I'm seventy, eighty, or ninety, what will I want to have accomplished in my lifetime?

2. If I had children and/or grandchildren, what would I want them to remember about me after I was gone?

3. When I die, what would I want my eulogy to say? What would I want people to say about me?

4. What do I need, or need to do, that would bring me the most pleasure, fulfillment, contentment, and satisfaction?

STEP 11: WRITE YOUR PERSONAL MISSION STATEMENT

By now you have done a tremendous amount of work in building self-awareness and discovering your true authentic self. Hopefully you've gained insight into your behaviors, thoughts, and emotions. You've identified your values, strengths and weaknesses, passions, fears, accomplishments and failures, and motivators. And you've done work to better understand your upbringing and life experiences, and what you want from life.

In business, companies summarize who they are and their intentions with a mission statement. This gives the company direction and a consistent message in everything it does. Essentially, a company's mission statement is like its constitution. Now that you understand a bit more about yourself, you can apply all the knowledge you've gained and bring it together to develop your own personal mission statement.

Unlike what you uncovered in **Step 10: Determine What You Want**, which focused on what you want out of life, your mission statement should talk about the type of person you want to be and how you want to contribute to life. It should speak about the characteristics and qualities by which you want to live. Your mission statement should be something you can identify with and of which you can be proud. It should be reflective of your authentic self, and not other people's beliefs or values. It should inspire you and, if done well, should provide you with direction and motivation to be proactive. Ideally your mission statement should transcend all the dimensions of well-being—the social, career, emotional, physical, intellectual, and spiritual dimensions. See below for some examples of mission statements:

- I will see the best in others, and the best in every situation. I will not be judgmental. I will ensure that I practice gratitude. I will take care of my body and my health. I will treat others as I hope to be treated. And I will live life to the fullest.

- I will put my best into everything that I do. I will live with passion and choose activities, friendships, and relationships that bring out the best in me. I will bring out the best in others, and I will give my time and energy to the things I value.

- I want to promote a healthy environment wherever I go. I want to encourage healthy and supportive relationships with and between others. I want to be true to myself and help others be true to themselves. I want to overcome fears that limit me from growing and experiencing all that life has to offer.

Step 11 Tasks

Using the **My Mission Statement Worksheet** in **Part III: The New You Journal** as a template, describe what you believe is your mission in life. Try to keep your statement to no longer than a few sentences or a short paragraph. Keep in mind all the positive things you just reflected on: your values, your passions, your strengths, and what you want, while answering these questions:

- What characteristics and qualities do I want to live by?

- How do I want to contribute to the world?

- What kind of influence do I want to have?

- What legacy would I like to leave?

If you find you could use a little more guidance, a great resource for building your personal mission statement is FranklinCovey's Mission Statement Builder at www.franklincovey.com/msb/.

KEY FACTORS FOR SUCCESS DURING STAGE 2

1. OBJECTIVE ANALYSIS

Self-awareness and self-discovery require a good level of objective analysis. Unlike subjectivity, which draws on emotional responses to evaluate situations, objective analysis means looking at situations through a lens of rational thinking. Essentially, you use data to understand situations, experiences, and circumstances. Although you will be required to identify your emotions during many of the exercises throughout Stage 2, objectivity will help you to understand them in a nonjudgmental way, so you can analyze your past on a deeper, more thoughtful level.

When we look at things through an emotional lens, our thoughts can become clouded regarding what is real and what isn't. Our emotions are very powerful, and as a result, they can cause us to latch onto feelings and become stuck rather than find productive ways to deal with negativity or hurtful experiences from our past. Objectivity keeps us out of an emotional, reactive place and enables exploration of situations so we can better understand them in a clear and rational way.

As a result of her father's infidelities, Elizabeth's parents got divorced when she was very young. Although she seemed to handle the divorce relatively OK as a child, the pain of it inevitably started to present itself when she started to date. She struggled with romantic relationships, finding it difficult to trust her boyfriends, often ending relationships prematurely. She judged marriage as a worthless institution. Elizabeth felt, after all, that her parents' marriage had failed miserably, and that men would inevitably cheat no matter what.

At the age of thirty-seven, after years of failed relationships, Elizabeth met Jake. Jake seemed different from any other man she had ever been with, yet she still had a difficult time committing to him. When he proposed, she told him that she didn't believe in marriage, and as a result, didn't see the point in staying together. Jake truly loved Elizabeth and was very persistent. He didn't want to give up so quickly. He managed to convince her to go to couples counseling with him.

When their therapy started, Elizabeth began with a very judgmental and negative attitude toward marriage. She didn't see how she could ever be convinced that it was something she would want for herself. After a couple of months of sessions, however, Elizabeth and Jake's therapist managed to get Elizabeth to move from an emotionally reactive mindset into an objectively analytical one. He helped her to see how the reality of her parents' divorce impacted her emotionally, behaviorally, and mentally. She eventually realized that the pain she harbored from her father's infidelities and from the divorce caused her to develop self-confidence issues, trust issues, and commitment issues. In looking at the situation objectively, she was able to put the emotion and judgment aside, and could see it was limiting her from living a potentially beautiful and happy life with Jake.

After another month or so, Elizabeth developed a new mindset toward love and finally accepted Jake's proposal of marriage. Today, over ten years later, they are still together and happy, and they have two beautiful children. Elizabeth continues to practice objective analysis when problems or difficulties arise. She is thankful that she has learned to look at situations from a rational perspective.

Staying in an emotional place limited Elizabeth, keeping her from finding true happiness. However, when she was able to move toward an objective analytical mindset, she was able to successfully step back and fully understand the implications of her life experiences. This inevitably allowed her to successfully visualize and plan a life that was meaningful.

The point of self-discovery is to gain a deeper understanding of yourself and what makes you the person you are. Avoid passing judgment on yourself or your experiences, and although you should identify your emotions, attempt to be rational in assessing their meaning and their source. Finally, let go of the pain as much as possible. What *is* is. What *was* was. Learn from it so you can move past it.

2. HONESTY

Honesty is an important characteristic in general, but in Stage 2, it helps you to discover your most authentic self.

We are often afraid to confront our feelings and emotions. Instead, we may play recordings in our mind that are dishonest about how we really feel or what the situation is or was really like. Pretending you don't feel what you do or that hurtful experiences from the past haven't impacted you keeps you in a place of denial. As painful as it may be, it is important to be aware of your feelings and thoughts about the past so you can use that information in helping you to build a better future.

Being honest with yourself provides the following benefits:

1. **It Reinforces That You Are OK:** Being honest means you are able to accept your faults and life circumstances and feel OK with who you are and your personal history. Dishonesty, however, reinforces the idea that you aren't good enough, that you somehow need to be different. It sets up an unhealthy dynamic that you have to pretend to be someone different in order to be OK. We all have demons and baggage, and yours doesn't make you any different or any less valuable as a person. You are OK as you are.

2. **It Encourages Self-Esteem:** True self-esteem stems from an ability to accept yourself and love yourself, as you are, warts and all. The more you are able to do this, the more you will cultivate a healthy self-esteem and level of self-confidence. The more you lie to yourself, however, or pretend you are someone other than who you really are, the more you undermine it.

3. **It Enables Change:** Real change requires that you come from a place of honesty. If you can acknowledge the truth of your past and the circumstances of your life, you can move past the hurt or pain so you can make changes to feel happier and enjoy a better tomorrow. When you aren't honest with yourself, however, you hinder your ability to change. Unless you can honestly understand yourself, you can't accurately define what you want for the future, making it difficult to create a clear and authentic path toward change. Self-awareness is the foundation for change.

All the work that you have done in **Stage 2: Discover Yourself** is going to be instrumental to your success moving forward. In order to change for the better, you will want to factor all you learned during the self-discovery process into your vision and plan for your future. Doing so will make your personal reinvention and the changes you make much more genuine, putting you on a path to achieve and live the life you really want and deserve. As you continue through each of the following stages, revisit the work you've done during this stage. It will continue to impact your work and the decisions you make throughout the process.

Stage 2 Summary

Stage 2 is focused on discovering your authentic self so you can design and plan a personal reinvention that is most beneficial to you.

Step 1: Define Your Values. Defining your values will provide you with the basis from which your reinvention can start.

Step 2: Identify Your Strengths and Acknowledge Your Weaknesses. Identifying your strengths will be important in creating a plan that capitalizes on your talents, while understanding your weaknesses will help you know what to avoid integrating.

Step 3: Identify and Address Your Fears. Identify your fears, both past and current, so you can find ways to overcome them and take more risks to build the life you want.

Step 4: Identify Your Passions. Identifying your passions will be helpful in creating a plan that continues to motivate you.

Step 5: Celebrate Your Accomplishments. Your accomplishments will act as reminders of what you are capable of so that you stay inspired throughout the process.

Step 6: Learn from Your Failures. Failure is inevitable for even the most successful of individuals. It should be seen as a positive experience that affords you an opportunity to learn and grow.

Step 7: Determine Your Motivators. Your motivators will be used to help keep you motivated and inspired throughout your reinvention.

Step 8: Understand Your Upbringing. Understanding your upbringing provides insights into why you are the way you are and how your upbringing has influenced your life. This will help you to evaluate what is truly important to you as an individual rather than what might have been passed down to you or expected of you.

Step 9: Evaluate Other Life Experiences. Life experiences outside of the home have also had a large impact on you and your life. Understanding these will help you to gain a deeper understanding of who you are.

Step 10: Determine What You Want. Define what you want out of life so that you can begin visualizing your ideal future.

Step 11: Write Your Personal Mission Statement. A mission statement provides you with a personal constitution of how you want to live your life and the type of person you want to be.

Principle of Change #2

SELF-AWARENESS IS THE FOUNDATION FOR CHANGE.

STAGE 3: DESIGN YOUR VISION

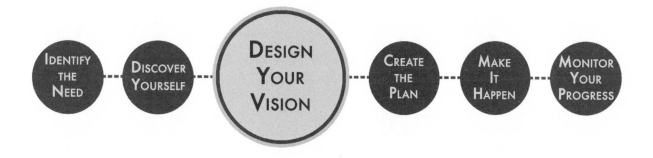

IDENTIFY THE NEED · DISCOVER YOURSELF · DESIGN YOUR VISION · CREATE THE PLAN · MAKE IT HAPPEN · MONITOR YOUR PROGRESS

YOUR VISIONS WILL BECOME CLEAR ONLY WHEN YOU CAN LOOK INTO YOUR OWN HEART. WHO LOOKS OUTSIDE, DREAMS; WHO LOOKS INSIDE, AWAKES.

—C. G. JUNG

When a company is interested in driving change within its organization, it creates a vision statement. The vision is a declaration of where the company hopes to be in the future and provides the organization with direction and the motivation to make changes that will get it there. Just as vision statements help companies, they can also help individuals reach their goals.

In **Stage 3: Design Your Vision**, you are going to focus on developing your personal vision statement, which will guide you on your path to personal reinvention. A personal vision is a picture of your future. This picture gives direction to the changes you want to make and can be used as a tool to inspire you to move forward in aligning your actions with specific end goals in mind. Without a vision of the future, efforts toward change lack meaning and purpose, and instead of forging ahead, you might find yourself aimlessly waffling through life. A vision provides the clarity needed so that decisions are easily made and action can be taken that supports reaching future goals. This brings us to our third Principle of Change:

Principle of Change #3
VISION GIVES CHANGE MEANINGFUL DIRECTION.

Lastly, a vision empowers you to take control of your future. For it to be effective, however, it is essential that you design it with a commitment toward the work and effort required to see your vision come to fruition.

Stage 3 Action Steps

The work you completed during **Stage 2: Discover Yourself** was very intensive and will prove to be very powerful as you continue on your path to personal reinvention. The information you uncovered should have provided you with deeper insight as to why you might be seeing or experiencing the signs you uncovered during **Stage 1: Identify the Need**. To create your vision, you will reference both your findings from Stage 1 and the work you just completed in Stage 2. Doing so will help you develop a vision that is authentic to your true self.

STEP 1: VERIFY WORK FROM STAGE 1

Revisit the work you did in Stage 1 to verify that the signs you identified are consistent with your findings from Stage 2. Although this may seem redundant, you originally identified signs based on a great deal of intuition in Stage 1. With your gained insight from Stage 2, however, you can now evaluate your interest in change from a more rational perspective and a deeper understanding of who you are.

Step 1 Tasks

Well-Being Self-Assessment

Refer to the **Dimensions of Well-Being Self-Assessment** you completed in Stage 1 for the following activities:

1. Based on what you now know about yourself from the self-discovery process, verify your initial assessment of how important each dimension of well-being is to your overall happiness. If the work you did in Stage 2 gives you new perspective and you feel you'd like to modify your initial ratings for any of the dimensions, rerate them now.

2. Based on your findings from Stage 2, review the ratings you provided for your current level of satisfaction within each dimension of well-being. Again, if you need to revise your ratings, do so.

3. Verify that the dimensions of well-being in which you saw potential for change are still applicable. If you feel you need to modify your initial responses, do so.

Although each dimension of well-being is important to your overall happiness, those dimensions you find most important yet feel most dissatisfied with are the dimensions on which you want to focus. You may have only one dimension in particular that stands out as needing change, or there may be a couple. Whatever the case, these are officially your Dimensions for Personal Reinvention.

Personal Signs of Change

4. Refer to the **Personal Signs of Change Matrix** you completed in Stage 1. Based on your findings from Stage 2, do you believe the signs you originally identified are still correct?

5. If not, revise as necessary.

Causes of Signs

Review your responses in the **Rational and Emotional SOS Assessment** and the **Physical SOS Assessment** from Stage 1, and evaluate your findings by completing the following tasks:

1. Based on your findings from Stage 2, do you think the possible causes you originally cited for your signs are accurate?

2. If you see a need to revise your work, do so now.

Step 2: Map the Gap

Your next step is to map the gap between where you are today and where you want to be tomorrow. Mapping this gap will help you start to see where the opportunities are to create change and will be the basis from which you design your vision.

Step 2 Tasks

For each Dimension for Personal Reinvention you want to address, use the **Personal Reinvention Gap Map** in **Part III: The New You Journal** as a template to do the following exercises:

1. Under the column titled "Today," list all the signs—rational, physical, and emotional—you verified during Step 1.

2. In the column labeled "Tomorrow," describe how things would be if all the signs you listed under "Today" were gone.

You now should have a fresh, clean slate from which to begin your personal reinvention and should see a clear, simple picture of where you are today and where you hope to be in the future.

STEP 3: PICTURE YOUR IDEAL TOMORROW

Referencing the work from both Step 1 and Step 2, you are going to paint a picture of the future so you can develop a more structured, formal vision statement.

Step 3 Tasks

Use the **My Ideal Tomorrow Worksheet** in **Part III: The New You Journal** as a template to respond to the following as it applies to your life as a whole:

1. Describe in detail what your ideal life would be like. Don't restrict yourself or worry about the length of your description. Also, don't worry about any one particular dimension, just focus on the big picture for now. To help, ask yourself the following:

    *   If I could remove all my fears, worries, concerns or anxieties, and current obstacles, what would my ideal life look like?

- How would I feel?

- What would I do?

- Where would I live?

- Where would I work?

- What would be important to me?

- What would my family be like? My friends? My colleagues?

Once you've completed the narrative, let the picture of your ideal life sink into your mind. Imagine what it would feel like and how happy you'd be. Next, you are going to do the same exercise for each of the dimensions you've targeted as your Dimensions for Personal Reinvention. Using the **My Ideal Tomorrow Worksheet** template, start a new page for each dimension and do the following:

2. Describe in detail how you envision your ideal state to be within the dimension of [insert specific dimension of concern].

ROADBLOCK: FEELING LIMITED BY YOUR PAST

As we've learned during the self-discovery process, our past—both negative and positive—is a huge part of who we are. The future, however, is where we are headed. In order to create a vision, it is imperative that you don't allow limitations, or perceived limitations of past circumstances, to hinder you from creating a powerful vision that is optimal for your future.

1. **Shift Your Mindset:** When we get stuck in the negativity of the past, we become severely limited. We tell ourselves "I can't," "I shouldn't," or "It won't work." As Carol Dweck tells us in *Mindset*, this is a fixed mindset that limits our ability to grow and change. Start enabling a growth mindset by encouraging proactive behavior. Think "I can," "I should," or "How can I make it work?" These are much more productive thought processes that will enable and empower you to create the future you want.

2. **Focus on Your Strengths and Accomplishments:** When you feel limited, remind yourself of all the successes that you've had and what you've accomplished. Revisit the work you did in **Stage 2: Discover Yourself** around identifying your strengths and celebrating your accomplishments. These will give you a boost in self-confidence and inspire you to take on new challenges for the future.

3. **The Past Is the Past:** Remember, the negative things that happened in the past are in the past. You can't change them. That said, you can learn from those experiences and choose to deal with them in a positive, healthy way. Revisit the lessons learned from past failures, fears, or negative situations and remind yourself of how you overcame obstacles in order to achieve all that you have.

4. **Visualize the Positive:** Focusing on past limitations keeps us in an immobile place. See the future as a new chapter to recreate your reality and focus on what you want. This will help you to visualize positive outcomes, mobilizing you to make them a reality.

5. **You're in the Driver's Seat:** Remind yourself that the only person who can truly limit you and your future possibilities is you. You have the power to create whatever life you choose. You have the ability to choose happiness. You are in the driver's seat of your own life.

STEP 4: DRAFT YOUR VISION STATEMENT

Although you might be anxious to get this step done quickly, a truly solid and effective vision statement will not be created within a few minutes. You probably won't even develop it within an hour or two. The process will take time. Your vision is crucial to a successful personal reinvention, so it is important to give it the time it deserves.

A vision statement is a powerful tool because it allows you to build a life that is truly reflective of who you are and what you value. Ideally it should incorporate all aspects of life, and for purposes of your personal reinvention, should most definitely incorporate aspects that address your Dimensions for Personal Reinvention.

DEFINITION OVERVIEW

Although the *mission statement* you completed in Stage 2 may seem similar to a *vision statement*, they are quite different. Refer to the following definitions for clarity:

- **Mission Statement:** Your mission statement is a summary of who you are, what you stand for, your values, and your purpose in life. Most likely, this doesn't change very much throughout your life.

- **Vision Statement:** Your vision statement is a picture of your future in the next one to five years, which describes at a high level what you want to achieve and who and where you want to be in your life. Your vision generally changes as time passes and you achieve the goals you set.

A successful vision statement relies on several key qualities. As you draft yours, keep the following in mind:

1. **It's Desirable:** Your vision should appeal to you and your long-term interests, and should continue to inspire you to make positive change. There is no sense in describing a vision you have no interest in or don't like. It should be an improvement on today and should be something you are consistently motivated to achieve. Don't base your vision on a fad or trendy desires; instead, base it on desires that will hold true for the long term.

2. **It's Simple and Undeniably Clear:** Ambiguity in a vision statement won't effectively translate into meaningful goals. Your vision should be simple and provide you with clear direction. Be sure you can clearly articulate it so it continues to inspire, not overwhelm.

3. **It's Realistically Ambitious:** Your picture for the future should be balanced between what is clearly possible and what is ambitious. If your vision looks too much like your life today, or on the other hand is too outlandish, you will only set yourself up for disappointment down the road. Your vision should force you out of your comfort zone, but shouldn't stretch you beyond your capabilities.

4. **It's Measurable:** Your vision should be measurable, meaning you'll have a clear way of assessing whether you've achieved it. If it is too vague or ambiguous, you'll never feel as though you are working toward something important. You'll never see "the light at the end of the tunnel." In general, your vision should cover a one- to five-year time frame.

5. **It's Authentic:** Your vision should be consistent with your values and who you are. To create a vision that is anything but authentic will ultimately fail. Authenticity means staying consistent with your values, your beliefs, and your own desires. We are incapable of living and sustaining a life that isn't true to ourselves.

6. **It's End-Goal Specific:** Your vision shouldn't focus on the steps or milestones you need to take to achieve it, it should focus on the end state or the end goals. It should be a picture of what life will look like after all the work is done.

EXAMPLES OF VISION STATEMENTS

- *Ben: Within two years, I will be working as a pediatric nurse. I will have purchased a two-bedroom home and will have reconnected with three friends with whom I've lost touch.*

- *Michelle: Within five years I will be partner at my law firm. I will be fit and healthy, and will prioritize my health. My husband and I will be parents of two healthy children.*

- *Philip: Within one year I will lose fifty pounds and feel inspired to stay healthy for the long term. I will stay active by finding outdoor activities to enjoy in all kinds of weather. I will have healthy relationships with friends and loved ones, and will be able to eliminate or minimize the unhealthy relationships of my past.*

- *Janet: Within three years I will be president of the Rotary Club in my area. I will have instituted a continuing education program at the local high school to help local immigrants learn English. I will be head of the volunteer program at the local hospital.*

As you can see, these vision statement examples are specific to the individual, are realistically ambitious, are measurable over a one- to five-year time frame, and are simple. Each vision statement speaks directly to what the individual values.

Spend some time reviewing the work you did in **Step 2: Map the Gap** and **Step 3: Picture Your Ideal Tomorrow** to draft your vision for the future. You'll need to engage both your emotional side and your rational side during this process, because your rational side will have a sense for what is realistic and what is authentic to who you are while your emotional side will know what you will be continually motivated and inspired to accomplish.

Step 4 Tasks

Use the **My Vision Worksheet** in **Part III: The New You Journal** as a template, and respond to the following within the "Vision Statement Draft" section:

1. Ask yourself the following questions:

- Who do I want to be?

- What do I want to accomplish?

- What do I want to change?

- When do I want to achieve these things?

2. Consider the responses you gave in **Step 2: Map the Gap** and **Step 3: Picture Your Ideal Tomorrow,** and weave them into your vision statement.

3. Be sure to apply parameters around your vision so you can make it achievable and measurable, optimally within a one- to five-year time frame.

The process of writing a good vision statement will take time, and it might even be a little "messy." At some point you may think your vision is done, but after reviewing it a day or two later, you may realize you need to further tweak it. Or you may fully abandon your first couple of drafts or hash through a variety of revisions to get it right. Whatever your process, remember that the resulting vision statement will be what gives you clear direction for change. Remember, vision gives change meaningful direction.

STEP 5: EVALUATE FOR EFFECTIVENESS

The end goal in creating your vision is that it should be effective in helping you make the change you want. As John Kotter, the author of *Leading Change*, states, "An ineffective vision may be worse than no vision at all." An effective vision is going to incorporate all the key qualities listed in **Step 4: Draft Your Vision Statement**.

Step 5 Tasks

Once you've drafted your vision statement, evaluate its effectiveness for driving change. You'll want to make sure it adheres to the key qualities outlined in Step 4, and that it will truly inspire you and help you on your path to personal reinvention. Answer the following questions using the **Vision Effectiveness Evaluation** in **Part III: The New You Journal** as a template:

- Will this vision push me beyond today?

- Is it attainable and realistic?

- Will achieving this vision make me happier?

- Is it clear and simple?

- Will I continue to be inspired by this vision?

- Is it measurable?

- Is it consistent with my values and my mission statement?

- Is it authentic to me?

- Is it achievable within a one- to five-year time frame?

- Does this resonate with me? Do I like this vision?

If you've answered no to any of the above questions, it is an indication that your vision statement may need to be revised to make it more effective. Modify your statement until you feel it is where it needs to be. Ultimately, each of the answers you provide for the questions in the **Vision Effectiveness Evaluation** should be a yes.

Once you have finalized your vision and believe it is clear and well defined, write it down in the section "My Vision Statement for Personal Reinvention" of the **My Vision Worksheet**.

STEP 6: COMMUNICATE YOUR VISION

An outwardly expressed vision is more powerful than a vision that remains purely in your mind. Studies have shown that communicating your intentions helps to increase your sense of accountability in making things come to fruition, driving you toward achievement. The last step of **Stage 3: Design Your Vision** is to figure out how to express your vision in ways that are meaningful to you. Just because your vision is made up of words or phrases doesn't mean it has to remain in that format. If you'd like to have more fun with your vision beyond the words themselves, try something creative in how you represent it.

Step 6 Tasks

Once you've finalized your vision, communicate it through creative formats. Consider any and all of the following, or if you have a method of your own, by all means feel free to use it.

1. **Speak It:** Speak your vision out loud to yourself every day. Or, record yourself saying the words and replay it every day or at any time you need a reminder about what you are working toward. Hearing yourself express your vision on a regular basis will make your vision seem more real and give you ownership over making it happen.

2. **Frame It:** Whether you want to take a highly artistic approach or a more simplified, no-frills approach, consider making your vision a piece of artwork and framing it so you can visually appreciate it every day. If you use your computer to do the artwork, you can do very simple things. Play with fonts and colors, and incorporate some graphics to make it eye-catching. Once you have designed a beautiful image, print it at a large enough scale to frame it and appreciate it. Put it somewhere you can see every day.

3. **Share It:** If you are comfortable doing so, share your vision with people in your life who genuinely care about you. Expressing your vision to others helps to make you accountable. It also helps others better understand your priorities so they can support you and your goals to make change.

4. **Celebrate It:** If you know of other individuals who are trying to go through changes of their own, you may find it fun to celebrate the process together. Consider throwing a "Vision Party" at which you and others can share your personal visions. You might even spark some interest among friends and family who could benefit from making some change in their own lives as well.

5. **Board It:** Many people like to create vision boards, filled with images of where they hope to be in the future and what they'd like to accomplish. Visuals elicit emotional responses, and as a result are wonderful inspirational tools. It is important that your vision board is designed wisely, however, with intent and purpose. Otherwise, a vision board can become a visual smorgasbord of materialistic desires. Avoid the temptation to put up a smattering of images of pretty people and pretty things, as these images aren't really reflective of the deeper transformation or reinvention you might be considering. Instead, look for imagery that is more profound, relevant, and meaningful.

Vision Boards of the Twenty-First Century

If you haven't seen or heard of Pinterest.com, you might want to explore it. It is an online platform that allows you to create boards of images, organized by your interests. Think of it as the intersection of social media and scrapbooking. If you enjoy using other social-media platforms, Pinterest might be a very effective (and fun) way to create vision boards. A few benefits:

- You can change the images often.

- You can create a board for each dimension of well-being.

- There are no space limitations on a board.

- You don't need glue, tape, or any other messy materials.

- Your boards look attractive and organized.

- The boards take up no space in your home.

KEY FACTORS FOR SUCCESS DURING STAGE 3

1. A FUTURE-DRIVEN MENTALITY

Focusing on your future and what you want to accomplish is crucial to designing an optimal vision. Looking forward encourages more positive thoughts and feelings, since most of our negative thoughts are rooted in past disappointments or regrets. If you find yourself getting stuck in the past, remind yourself that tomorrow is a new day, and you'll have a new opportunity to create a better, more wonderful life.

2. A GROWTH MINDSET

As Carol Dweck explains in *Mindset*, in order to change and grow we need to have a growth mindset, as opposed to one that is fixed. A fixed mindset prevents us from making change, because it is rooted in a fear of failure. A growth mindset, however, embraces failure as part of the process of change and understands it is crucial to succeeding in the long run. Thinking "I can learn," "I can grow," "I can change," and "I can become more [fill in the blank]" is consistent with a growth mindset. On the other hand, thinking "I'm as good as I'm going to be," "I'm as smart as I am," "I'm as talented as I am," and "I can't change" is consistent with a fixed mindset. If at any point you feel that you *can't*, remind yourself that you *can*. Instead of fearing failure, try to embrace it as an inevitable part of the process that is instrumental to your long-term ability to succeed. Surround yourself with people who encourage growth and live by a standard of continual learning and growth themselves. Their growth mindset will rub off on you.

3. HEALTHY BAGGAGE HANDLING

The self-discovery process provided you with insights to help you understand what "baggage," or negative past experiences, you may be carrying emotionally and psychologically. Emotional baggage can reap both good and bad outcomes. Sometimes it inspires us to become better and pushes us to do great things, while at other times it may become a hindrance or an excuse for maintaining a life in the status quo.

> *Bill grew up with parents who worked tirelessly, but constantly scraped by to pay bills. They barely made it from paycheck to paycheck. When birthdays and holidays came around, Bill was lucky if he received a nice card. As Bill got older, he swore that he would create a better life for himself, and potentially for his family.*

> *Bill worked hard throughout high school, making him one of the top students of his class. He was accepted to a very competitive university on full scholarship, and still managed to work throughout his four years, anxious to build savings for when he graduated. Upon graduation he earned a highly coveted position with an international bank.*

After about ten years and numerous promotions, Bill was offered a position as an executive in private wealth management within a well-respected financial institution.

Craig, too, grew up in a very poor family. His parents struggled to make ends meet as well. Unfortunately, Craig let the circumstances from his upbringing limit him instead of inspire him. Even though he scored well on a lot of the standardized tests, he didn't apply himself very much in high school. When it was time for Craig to consider going to college, he decided not to and instead took a job with a local hardware store. His philosophy was this: "What's the point? I'm not going to get very far anyway. My parents worked really hard, and for what?" His path mirrored that of his parents. He remained relatively stagnant throughout his life, moving from menial job to menial job, making just enough money to get by.

Bill responded to the baggage from his past in a healthy and productive way. He used it as a way to inspire and motivate positive change for his own life. Craig, however, limited his future by believing it was predetermined by his past. Although Bill and Craig came from very similar backgrounds and essentially carried similar negative past experiences with them, how they chose to handle their situations differed.

How we deal with negative past circumstances and experiences is what can make or break our ability to make change for the better. If you find yourself struggling to deal with your baggage in a healthy way, consider the following tips:

1. **Accept It:** First, you need to acknowledge and accept past negative experiences. We all have them. Sure, you may not like your less-than-perfect past, but ignoring it or pretending it doesn't exist only puts you into a state of denial and can lead to more problems down the road. Accept that your negative experiences have had a role in your life. Embrace how they may have molded you and come to terms with the fact that, whether you like it or not, they are part of you.

2. **Reframe It:** Once you've come to terms with the reality, decide what you'd like to do about the emotional hurts, resentments, or perceived limitations you are carrying. Although our past is part of us, more likely than not we can work through a lot of it so we can move forward and get beyond it. In Bill's case, he used his negative past as a motivator to create a better future. To reframe your own experiences, ask:

- How can I use my past experiences to my advantage?

- What have I learned from them that can help me in the future?

This reframing exercise takes you out of a place of resentment and puts you in a more positive frame of mind. It also puts you in a place of proactive and rational thinking as opposed to a reactive and emotional place.

3. **Seek Professional Help When Necessary:** Seek the help of a professional if you are struggling with especially difficult situations or memories. Psychiatrists, psychologists, therapists, coaches, and social workers are professionals who can help you move beyond the hardships and unhealthy aspects of your past.

4. **Avoid Repeating History:** It is human nature to be drawn to people or situations that bring out old, comfortable habits. Relating to individuals who have similar history or baggage may seem natural; however, doing so can keep you in an immobile and negative place, stuck in the same ruts and behaviors of the past. Further, it may encourage toxic and unhealthy relationships. Be hyperaware of the circumstances you get into and avoid putting yourself in situations that let old, unhealthy habits resurface. Look for relationships that support healthier habits, and minimize those relationships that don't.

5. **Take Control:** It is easy to feel as though you are held hostage by your past. Remember, however, that the only way you fully lose control is if you give it up. Ultimately, you make your own decisions and have the power to control your destiny and to create the life you want. Although you may not be able to change the past, you most definitely can shape your future.

You now should have a complete and formalized vision statement, which you will use to guide you throughout your personal reinvention. This vision statement will be instrumental in creating your plan in Stage 4.

Stage 3 Summary

Stage 3 focuses on designing a vision for your future.

Step 1: Verify Work from Stage 1. Verify your work from Stage 1 to see if it is consistent with your findings from Stage 2. Make revisions if necessary.

Step 2: Map the Gap. Looking at the signs of significance you verified, map the gap between how things are today and how you want them to be in the future.

Step 3: Picture Your Ideal Tomorrow. Tell a story of how you want your future to look.

Step 4: Draft Your Vision Statement. Write your vision statement for the future.

Step 5: Evaluate for Effectiveness. Evaluate your vision statement to see if it adheres to the key qualities of an effective vision stipulated in Step 4. Revise as necessary.

Step 6: Communicate Your Vision. Find ways to outwardly communicate your vision so that it has a more formal and permanent role.

Principle of Change #3
VISION GIVES CHANGE MEANINGFUL DIRECTION.

STAGE 4: CREATE THE PLAN

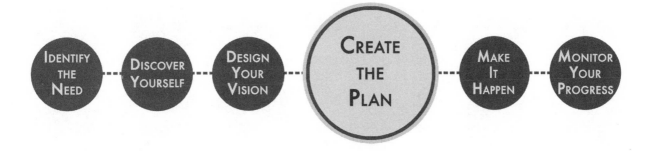

HE WHO FAILS TO PLAN IS PLANNING TO FAIL.

—WINSTON CHURCHILL

YOU JUST CREATED YOUR VISION for the future, and for a better, more improved you. Now you need to develop a plan that helps you make it happen. A plan is essential to taking your vision from dream to reality. It is the mechanism that provides you with a clear path to take action and to succeed. It involves setting major goals and milestones, and then designing a set of action steps that direct you toward meeting them. In essence, the vision is the *what* you want to achieve, and the plan is the *how* you will do it.

Your plan will need to address several key questions in order to be successful:

- What are the desired results?

- What will be required to achieve my goals?

- How will I achieve them?

- Where will I achieve them?

- When will I achieve them?

- Who will help me achieve them?

- How will I evaluate my progress?

- How will I reward my performance in completing milestones and tasks?

Your plan should address all these questions to ensure that it is effective in helping you make the changes you want. Planning for your personal reinvention will keep you moving on a path and will help you foresee potential obstacles so you can be better prepared if and when they present themselves. Winston Churchill said it well when he said, "He who fails to plan is planning to fail." His philosophy provides the basis for the fourth Principle of Change:

Principle of Change #4
PLANNING FOR CHANGE IS PLANNING TO SUCCEED.

Stage 4 Action Steps

Step 1: Identify Your End Goals

The vision you designed in **Stage 3: Design Your Vision** represents a big picture of where you want to be in one to five years. However, it also provides a starting point from which to develop end goals. To demonstrate, let's take a look at Michelle's vision statement provided in Stage 3:

Within five years I will be partner at my law firm. I will be fit and healthy, and will prioritize my health. My husband and I will be parents of two healthy children.

This vision statement actually includes four possible end goals, extending over a five-year period:

1. To become partner at the law firm.

2. To be healthy and fit.

3. To prioritize her health.

4. To have two children.

To begin the process of creating your plan, you are going to break down your vision into appropriate end goals. Although it is typically suggested that you develop "SMART" goals—those that are specific, measurable, actionable, relevant, and timely—to ensure they are effective, such a system doesn't appeal to your emotional side. As discussed, engaging your emotional side is crucial to staying motivated throughout the change process. As a result, you should make your end goals SMARTE with an *E*, which stands for *emotionally driven*:

- **Specific:** Your goals should be specific and clear so there is no room for interpretation. They must articulate exactly what is expected and attempt to answer the following questions. The clearer you can be, the less trouble you will have finding motivation. Ask yourself:

  o *What:* What do I want to accomplish?

  o *Why:* Why is the goal important?

  o *Who:* Who else do I need to help me accomplish the goal?

  o *Where:* Where will I achieve the goal?

  o *Which:* Which steps are necessary in order to accomplish the goal?

- **Measurable:** An effective goal must be measurable so you can evaluate your progress and know if you're headed in the right direction.

- **Actionable:** Goals should be actionable. If you can't do anything to actively work toward your goals, you risk setting yourself up for failure. Ask yourself:

  o Can I take action to work toward this goal?

  o Do I have the power to achieve it?

- **Relevant:** Your goals need to be closely aligned with your vision, your values, and what you hope to get out of life. Ask yourself:

  o Is this goal meaningful?

  o Is this goal consistent with my vision and personal mission statement?

  o Does this goal match my needs?

- **Timely:** No goal would be effective if it didn't have a time frame in which you hope to achieve it. This makes you accountable and pushes you toward completion by a specific date. Keep in mind that although your vision might span a longer time period, such as five years, your specific end goals may have their own individual target dates for completion within the overall time frame of the vision (three months, six months, one year, etc.). Ask yourself:

o   When do I want to accomplish these goals?

o   What can be accomplished in a month? Three months? Six months? A year?

- **Emotionally Driven:** You should have emotional drive to complete the goal and have a clear sense as to why it is important to you. The goal should create a fire in your belly, a passion that continually inspires you to make change toward your greater vision. If your goals hit you emotionally and grab you at a very deep level, you will be more likely to continue with your plan. Although the emotional aspect of a goal may not be represented in words per se, it should be apparent as to whether it resonates with you emotionally. Ask yourself:

o   Am I excited about this goal?

o   Do I feel inspired and motivated to accomplish this goal?

o   Will I be able to keep motivation levels high, all the way through to completion?

Although four end goals were preliminarily drafted for Michelle's vision on page 100, you can now see they don't quite fulfill all the SMARTE requirements. They do, however, provide a good starting point. If the SMARTE framework is applied to the same vision, it might result in the following end goals:

1. *Within five years, I will become partner at my law firm so that I can support my family and be considered a leader in the law industry. I will work with current partners and mentors to develop a plan to help me achieve this goal.*

2. *Within the next year I will lose twenty pounds by eating a healthier diet and exercising a minimum of three times each week.*

3. *Within six months, I will make my health a priority, by allotting three to five hours per week to exercise, maintaining a seven- to eight-hour nightly sleep schedule, and learning how to eat better when I travel.*

4. *Over the next four years, my husband and I will prepare for two children by developing a sound financial plan, looking for a neighborhood where we want to raise children, and purchasing a new home.*

As you can see, although the preliminarily drafted end goals seemed clear, the newly revised goals provide greater detail and specifics about how they will be accomplished, how they will be measured, and how long each will take. When it comes to making your goals relevant and emotionally inspiring, however, only you will know whether your goals accomplish this. These requirements are more qualitative and don't necessarily get written into the end goals themselves.

Step 1 Tasks

Using the **Big End Goals Worksheet** in **Part III: The New You Journal** as a template, conduct the following tasks:

1. With the SMARTE framework in mind, look at your vision and evaluate what seem to be the larger goals. In the column labeled "End Goals," write in each goal you identify. If you need to, refer to the example of Michelle to see how a vision might be broken down into end goals.

2. Review each of your end goals and evaluate whether they meet the SMARTE criteria. If they do, describe how under the column labeled "SMARTE Criteria."

3. If any of your end goals don't meet the SMARTE criteria, revise them so they do.

4. Repeat Tasks 1–3 until your vision is fully translated into SMARTE end goals.

STEP 2: RESEARCH WHAT IS REQUIRED

In order to achieve each of the end goals you have identified in Step 1, you will need to break them down into smaller goals, also called milestones, and action steps. To do so, you will need to understand what will be required to accomplish each goal. Once you have a solid understanding of what is entailed, you can then translate that into appropriate milestones and action steps. Be as thorough as possible, as the work you do in this step will be extremely important to the rest of the work you do during this stage.

Step 2 Tasks

In the column labeled "Key Requirements" of the **Big End Goals Worksheet**, provide information for each end goal around the following categories. Sample questions to consider have been provided for each category.

1. **Knowledge:** Do I need to learn anything new? Are there books I can read? Do I need to go back to school? How else might I gain the knowledge I need?

2. **Skills:** Do I need to develop or acquire any new skills? If so, how can I? Where and how might I practice those skills? Can I take lessons? Can I get an internship?

3. **Professional or External Help:** Do I need anyone else to help me in achieving my end goals? Do I need to hire any experts or professionals? If so, who?

4. **Money:** Will I need to spend any money to accomplish the goal? If so, how much? Is it something I can afford? If I have to go back to school, do I have the money? Are there scholarships available? If I need to hire anyone for professional help, how much do they cost?

5. **Time:** How much time do I need to dedicate toward achieving this goal? If there are other requirements, such as building knowledge or acquiring skills, how much time will it take to fulfill them?

6. **Other Resources:** What else might I need to accomplish my goal? Equipment? A professional network?

This information will be the basis for developing your milestones and action steps.

STEP 3: PRIORITIZE YOUR GOALS

As you may have discovered in **Step 2: Research What Is Required**, some end goals will be easier to accomplish than others. Additionally, some of them will be more impactful than others. When developing your personal plan for change, it will be helpful to prioritize end goals in such a way that your efforts are most productive and worthwhile. To do so, you will evaluate them around the following two qualities:

1. **Level of Impact:** It is probably fair to say that the end goals you've identified are meaningful. Yet, some might be more impactful to your happiness and personal reinventions than others. For instance, a goal may transcend several dimensions of well-being and not just one. Or, accomplishing certain goals will help you in accomplishing others, essentially making them prerequisites to your other goals. Only you really know what is most meaningful to you. For illustrative purposes, let's look at Michelle's four end goals, identified earlier. Of all of them, she might feel that focusing on her health and losing weight will be most impactful, because if she is in good health it will be easier to accomplish her other goals.

2. **Level of Difficulty:** Obviously, any goal you set out to accomplish is going to take work. If it doesn't, it probably isn't much of a goal in the first place. If a goal is tremendously difficult and requires a lot of effort, money, input from other people, or new skills, however, you might find it overwhelming to achieve. You may even run the risk of burnout. If reaching a goal is manageable, however, then the work you put in will feel well worth the effort, and better yet, might inspire you to continue making change. Based on the research you did in Step 2, you should have a good sense of how difficult each goal will be to reach.

Once you've assessed the impact and difficulty of your goals, you will be able to prioritize them. The goals that are of the highest impact to your vision and are the least difficult to accomplish should naturally be your highest priority. The goals you identify as being the lowest in impact and the most difficult should be the lowest priority. Refer to the *Prioritization Matrix* on page 122 for an illustration of this.

Step 3 Tasks

Adding to the work you did on the **Big End Goals Worksheet**, do the following:

1. For each end goal, rate its level of impact on a scale of 1 to 10 (1 is the lowest impact, 10 is the highest) and enter the rating in the column titled "Impact." You'll want to ask yourself:

- How great an impact will this end goal have on my vision?

- Will this goal bring about a big difference in my happiness?

- Will achieving this goal bring about desired results?

- Is this goal a prerequisite to any of my other goals?

2. Reference the work you did in **Step 2: Research What Is Required** to answer the following questions for each goal. Based on your answers, rate the goal's level of difficulty on a scale of 1 to 10 (1 is the least difficult, 10 is most) and enter the rating in the column titled "Difficulty":

- How much effort will it take to achieve this goal?

- Will it require that I learn a lot of new skills or develop new behaviors?

- Will it require that I recruit the help of others?

- Will it utilize my strengths or weaknesses?

- Will it cost a lot of money?

- How much control do I have in achieving this goal?

3. Any end goals rated 1 to 5 in impact are considered low-impact. Any rated above 5 are considered high-impact. Similarly, any end goals rated 1 to 5 in difficulty are considered low in difficulty, while any above 5 are high in difficulty. Summarize your ratings in the column labeled "Priority" using the following designations: High Impact/Low Difficulty (H/L); High Impact/High Difficulty (H/H); Low Impact/Low Difficulty (L/L); and Low Impact/High Difficulty (L/H).

4. Use the **Prioritization Matrix Worksheet** in **Part III: The New You Journal** as your template. Write the number of each end goal (from the **Big End Goals Worksheet**) in the quadrant that correlates with the goal's level of impact and difficulty. Goals rated H/L go in "High Priority; H/H goals go in "Midpriority," L/L in "Easy Wins," and L/H in "Not Worth It."

5. The goals you've placed in the "High Priority" quadrant are your first-priority goals. Any goals that fall into the "Not Worth It" quadrant should be avoided altogether; they will take too much work and will provide very little return on your investment of time and energy. The goals you've placed in the "Easy Wins" and the "Midpriority" quadrants of the matrix need to be further evaluated.

6. "Easy Wins" might be worth doing even though they may not be tremendously impactful, because you will gain a sense of achievement from accomplishing them. Achievement, even on a small scale, still creates enthusiasm and motivation to continue working toward your overall vision. On the other hand, the "Midpriority" goals will be much more impactful, even though they will take greater effort. In the end, you have to decide what is more important to you.

7. In the section titled "Prioritized End Goals" at the bottom of the **Prioritization Matrix Worksheet**, list your end goals in order of priority.

ROADBLOCK: INDECISION

Henry Ford once said, "Indecision is often worse than wrong action." When creating your plan, you may find it difficult to commit to various goals or a direction in which you want to head. Many of us suffer from a need for certainty, a need to be right, or assurance that things will turn out the way we want. Indecision often stems from a fear that we will make a "wrong" decision that will produce unfavorable results. Not making a decision, however, can cause a lot of wasted time, anxiety, and stress, which in the end sabotages our ability to succeed at making change and acts as a roadblock to finding happiness.

When we look at decisions through a lens of "right" or "wrong," we limit ourselves. Although keeping options open may seem like the best idea, it can often result in stagnation, meaning we don't experience anything at all. It is interesting to note that studies have shown that regret, an unarguably negative emotion, is more often a result of lack of action than "mistaken" or "wrong" action. Even a perceived wrong decision can bring about better results than no decision at all, as it can teach us and guide us in making better decisions for the future. Reduce indecision with the following tips:

1. **Prioritize around Your Values:** Your values are the basis from which you can become more decisive. When confronted with a situation or decision you need to make, weigh your options and prioritize them against your values so they best align with what is important to you.

2. **Limit Your Options:** Studies show that the more options we have, the less likely we are to make a decision. If you find that you are overwhelmed by all the choices you have, try narrowing down your options so that you have less "noise" and can focus on a few things at a time.

3. **Let Go of Perfection:** If your indecision is a result of looking for a perfect outcome, remember there is no such thing as perfect, "right" or "wrong," or "good" or "bad." Also, keep in mind that making any decision often provides more benefits as compared to making no decision at all: you will make some sort of progress, may learn more about yourself, and may learn lessons for the future.

4. **Keep Your Decisions Personal:** Sometimes we struggle to make decisions because we worry about what others will think of us. For instance, if you choose a job because it is considered prestigious, even though you don't have interest in the work, you are making a decision predicated on the opinions of others and not what is best for you. Remind yourself of your values and what is important to you, and aim to make decisions based on these.

5. **Build Your Self-Confidence:** The inability to make decisions can often be a result of a lack in self-confidence. It is important to trust your intuition and believe in yourself to take an appropriate course of action. You have the power to create the life you want. Believe in yourself to make it the best life possible.

6. **Turn Challenges into Opportunities:** If your indecision stems from the idea that certain courses of action present challenges or are difficult, look at ways to turn those challenges into opportunities. For instance, if your goal is to switch careers but you lack the necessary skills, think of it as an opportunity to take classes and study something in which you have interest and passion. Not only will the knowledge and new skills you develop be helpful to your potential new career, but going back to school may also help you expand your network and find a job.

7. **Gain Outside Perspective:** Although you want to ensure your decisions are predicated on your own goals and needs, it may be helpful to get outside perspective from a mentor, a friend you trust, or someone who knows you well. They may be able to shed some light on making a decision.

THE PRIORITIZATION MATRIX

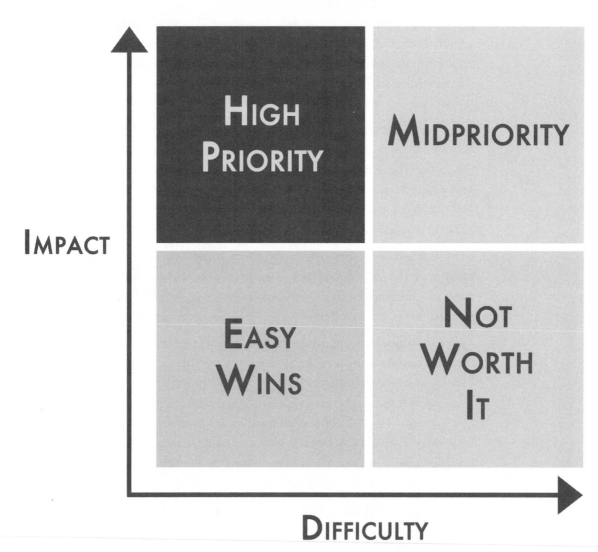

STEP 4: BREAK GOALS INTO MILESTONES AND ACTION STEPS

Your plan for personal reinvention requires that each end goal be broken down into milestones and action steps. Milestones are essentially smaller goals, and action steps are the activities you need to complete in order to accomplish them.

Breaking down end goals in this manner provides numerous benefits. First, changes will seem much more manageable. Second, smaller goals allow you to accomplish things more regularly and in shorter periods of time so that you stay motivated. And third, with each accomplished goal, you'll feel closer to achieving your vision.

Each milestone you identify should follow the same SMARTE format as your big end goals. They should be specific, measurable, actionable, relevant (to the end goal), timely, and—of course—emotionally driven. The metrics you use for milestones, however, should be smaller than those of your end goals. And your time frames to accomplish your milestones should be shorter.

> *Jason's end goal was to lose about twenty pounds in four months, culminating on December 1. Instead of letting the number twenty overwhelm him, he broke his end goal down into smaller milestones of weight loss over shorter periods of time. He realized that twenty pounds over four months equated to about five pounds per month. As a result, he identified his milestones to be: lose five pounds by August 31, lose another five pounds by September 30, lose another five pounds by October 31, and finally, lose the last five pounds by November 30. Losing five pounds per month seemed much easier to achieve than losing the full twenty. As each month passed, Jason felt a great sense of accomplishment with every five pounds he shed, keeping him motivated throughout all four months so he could successfully achieve his end goal.*

ROADBLOCK: Inability to See beyond the Big Picture

It's crucial to visualize the steps you need to take in order to achieve a goal. If you struggle to break bigger goals into smaller milestones, consider the following:

1. **Pretend You Are a Teacher:** Sometimes it is helpful to step back from a situation so you can see it more clearly. Imagine teaching a child or a teenager about your goals, as if they would be the ones making the changes. Think about how you might help them make it more manageable. How would you help them break it down?

2. **Do Research:** We live in an age when information is readily available at the simple click of a button. Do research on the Internet, or read books that address the changes you are interested in making. If, for instance, you want to make changes on improving your outlook, read up on how to develop a positive mindset and ways to reframe the way you think about things.

3. **Get Help:** Solicit the help of friends, family members, or colleagues to help you think through what might be required to reach your goals. It may also be helpful to speak to others who are experts or have gone through similar changes. For instance, if you want to develop more self-confidence, speak with people you know who exude confidence or who seem more confident than they used to be.

4. **Test Things Out:** Sometimes a path doesn't become clear unless we test things out first. For instance, if you are interested in making change within the dimension of spirituality, you might want to start the process by visiting different houses of worship or trying a variety of spiritual activities, such as yoga or meditation, to understand what resonates with you the most. Testing things may give you better insight into what will be entailed to accomplish your end goals and milestones.

DEFINITION OVERVIEW

At this point, you've been reading about a variety of terms—*goals*, *milestones*, and *action steps*—that may seem similar. If you feel as though all these terms are blending together, refer to the following definitions for clarity:

Goals: Goals or end goals are what you want to specifically achieve in order to make your vision come to fruition. They follow a SMARTE format.

Milestones: Milestones are smaller goals you accomplish (which also follow a SMARTE format) to help you toward achieving bigger end goals.

Action Steps: Action steps are the specific steps, tasks, or activities you take in order to reach your milestones and goals.

Step 4 Tasks

Using the **End Goals, Milestones, and Action Steps Worksheet** in **Part III: The New You Journal** as a template, develop a detailed plan with milestones and action steps for each major end goal you've prioritized in **Step 3: Prioritize Your Goals**. Please note that although the template has a set number of entry lines, your plan should be customized to your needs. This is just an illustrative template to help you structure your plan.

1. Milestones should be bite-size chunks of your larger goal (e.g., Jason's weight-loss example). You should feel and believe they are achievable and that you can succeed. If a milestone feels overwhelming, then it is too big and should be broken down further. Starting with your highest priority goals, break each down into smaller milestones. Be sure to make each milestone SMARTE—specific, measurable, actionable, relevant, timely, and emotionally driven. Aim for shorter time frames for each, such as a week or two or a month or two. List each milestone you identify under the "Milestones" header of the **End Goals, Milestones, and Action Steps Worksheet**.

2. For each milestone, identify appropriate action steps required. Go back and reference the work you did in **Step 2: Research What Is Required** for each of your end goals, and apply the same process to developing your action steps. List the action steps you identify under the "Action Steps" section of the **End Goals, Milestones, and Action Steps Worksheet**.

3. For each action step and milestone you've identified, apply what you've learned from **Stage 2: Discover Yourself**. Specifically, look at ways in which you might be able to incorporate your strengths, your passions, and your motivators. Revisit the examples of Tony and Joy; Tony utilized his strength as a good tennis player and Joy used her passion for reading books to stay motivated in reaching their weight-loss goals. Apply your own strengths, passions, and motivators to your plan.

4. Repeat Tasks 1, 2, and 3 for each end goal you have prioritized.

Although the plan you just developed may change over time, especially as you progress through it, it is an excellent starting point from which you can begin your reinvention.

Step 5: Assign Time Frames to Goals and Milestones

Once you know all the end goals, milestones, and action steps required to achieve your vision, you will want to create a time frame in which to accomplish them. By no means does the process have to be linear. You may find there are end goals or milestones you can work toward in parallel with others. For instance, if you have an end goal involving weight loss and an end goal of improving your relationships, there is no reason you can't work on both at the same time. Or, you may have an end goal that requires a variety of milestones and action steps to be done in tandem, such as going back to school and finding an internship so you can embark on a new career. Or, you may find that some milestones or goals can only be achieved once others have been tackled. The most important thing is that you stay realistic about how much change you can take on at once, and how you can most effectively progress in achieving your goals. If you can manage or handle a lot without the risk of burnout, then feel free to do so. If, however, you are best when you focus on one thing at a time, then consider that in developing your time frame.

THE IMPORTANCE OF SHRINKING THE CHANGE

In *Switch: How to Change Things When Change Is Hard*, Chip and Dan Heath talk about the importance of "shrinking the change." They note that "people find it more motivating to be partly finished with a longer journey than to be at the starting gate of a shorter one." They go on to explain that "you'll start to take pride in your accomplishments...and that pride and confidence will build on itself."

You can look at each of your end goals as big changes and your milestones as smaller ones. These smaller changes are highly beneficial to any effort you make, because they accomplish several important things:

You Will Stay Motivated: With each small success, you will feel inspired to complete bigger goals, as well as feeling more successful, more confident, and headed in a good direction. Bigger goals will seem less daunting, and the momentum you build will help carry you through more challenging moments.

They Make Change More Manageable: Every large goal is essentially made of many smaller goals. Shrinking changes allows you to take things one step at a time so the changes seem less daunting.

They Provide Opportunities to Fine-Tune Your Plan: Setting up milestones allows you to regularly assess if something isn't working or if a shorter-term milestone becomes impossible to achieve. You can adjust your plan in a much more efficient and timely manner.

They Establish a Well-Defined Path: Identifying milestones will put you on a clear path that is consistent in direction and purpose. It will keep you moving forward, and will help eliminate potential wavering.

Step 5 Tasks

In the column titled "Due Date" in the **End Goals, Milestones, and Action Steps Worksheet**, fill in a target date for the completion of each end goal and milestone. Be realistic in your expectations so that you don't try to complete goals or milestones too quickly.

- You may find that some of your milestones or end goals, once achieved, will need to be maintained on an ongoing basis. For instance, let's say a milestone is to go to the gym four times a week. At some point the hope would be that you would be able to maintain this level of activity. In this case, make the target date the date by which you hope you are able to consistently maintain your goal.

- You could also consider putting in target dates for your action steps, but be careful not to overcontrol or overplan each detail to the point that it becomes burdensome or inflexible. Depending on the end goal or milestone, action steps might need to be completed on a more organic level. Use your best judgment.

CREATING MILESTONES AND ACTION STEPS—AN EXAMPLE

Ilene is interested in reinventing her career by making a switch from technology sales to marketing within the biotechnology industry. Her end goal is to gain a marketing position at a biotech company within six months. In order to make this goal a reality, she creates a plan by breaking her bigger goal down into several smaller and more manageable milestones:

1. Send resumes to ten companies within four weeks.

2. Go on at least four interviews within two months.

3. Secure at least two offers within four months.

4. Obtain a new job within six months.

Next, Ilene identifies action steps for each of her milestones. For her first milestone—send resumes to ten companies within four weeks—Ilene identifies the following action steps:

1. Draft resume and cover letter.

2. Send resume and cover letter to five people for review and feedback.

3. Edit both based on feedback.

4. Repeat steps 1 and 2 until confident the résumé is ready.

5. Research companies within the local area.

6. Network with friends, family, and business colleagues who might have connections at local biotech companies.

7. Contact companies to identify who should receive résumé and cover letter.

8. Send out résumés and cover letters to identified individuals.

Finally, Ilene identifies target dates for completion for each of her milestones and end goals and, in this case, for her action steps.

Ilene's detailed plan makes it much easier to tackle the work required to achieve her goal. She can make progress one step at a time, and will feel a sense of accomplishment along the way. With every step made, she will be closer to completion. Refer to the *Sample End Goals, Milestones, and Action Steps Plan* on page 134 to see how Ilene's plan might look within the template provided in *Part III: The New You Journal.*

Sample End Goals, Milestones, and Action Steps Plan

End Goals	Milestones		Action Steps	Due Date
		1		
		1a	Draft resume and cover letter.	4/7
Gain a marketing position within the biotech industry within six months.	Send resumes to ten biotech companies within four weeks.	1b	Send resume and cover letter to five people I trust for review and feedback.	4/8
		1c	Edit both based on feedback.	4/12
		1d	Repeat steps 1 and 2 until I feel confident my résumé is ready.	4/20
		1e	Research companies I'm interested in within my local area.	4/12
		1f	Network with friends, family, and business colleagues who might have connections at biotech companies.	4/15
		1g	Contact companies to identify who should receive resume and cover letter.	4/20
		1h	Send resumes and cover letters.	4/28
			Milestone Due Date	**4/28**

2		2a	_____	_____
	Go on at least four interviews within two months.	2b	_____	_____
		2c	_____	_____
		2d	_____	_____
		2e	_____	_____
		Milestone Due Date		**5/31**
3	Secure at least two offers within four months.	3a	_____	_____
		3b	_____	_____
		3c	_____	_____
		3d	_____	_____
		3e	_____	_____
		Milestone Due Date		**7/31**
4	Obtain a new job within six months.	4a	_____	_____
		4b	_____	_____
		4c	_____	_____
		4d	_____	_____
		4e	_____	_____
		Milestone Due Date		**9/30**
		END GOAL DUE DATE		**9/30**

STEP 6: BUILD IN A REWARDS SYSTEM

At this point you have fleshed out a pretty extensive plan for your personal reinvention. You've identified all your goals, milestones, and action steps, and their respective time frames and metrics. Now, you'll want to identify appropriate rewards to celebrate each of the milestones and goals you accomplish.

Hopefully your inspiration to reach your goals is because doing so will bring you a greater level of happiness and allow you to be your best self. As a result, the rewards you build into your plan shouldn't necessarily act as incentives but instead as symbols of appreciation and recognition for the work you put into your achievements. Formally acknowledging your accomplishments through a set of rewards instills a feeling of progress and success, inspiring you to continue on the path that you created.

Step 6 Tasks

Use the **End Goals, Milestones, and Action Steps Worksheet** to do the following tasks:

1. Look at each of your end goals and milestones and think about a reward you'd like to receive for achieving them. The rewards you choose are completely up to you, but ideally they should continue to emotionally inspire you. Maybe you've wanted to take a trip. Maybe it is a celebration with loved ones. Maybe it is a purchase you've been putting off for some time. Regardless, you should look forward to your reward as much as the feeling you will have in accomplishing the goal or milestone itself.

2. In the column titled "Reward," fill in the reward you have identified for each milestone and end goal.

STEP 7: BUILD IN REGULAR CHECKPOINTS

In order to monitor your progress in Stage 6, you will want to build in regular checkpoints to assess how you are doing with your plan. Checkpoints should be frequent enough that you don't find yourself on an incorrect path for too long, but spread out enough so you have sufficient time to attempt a number of the action steps outlined and to see if they are working.

If you have a lot of smaller action steps that don't require a tremendous amount of effort, you might want to build in checkpoints more frequently. If, however, reaching a milestone requires a variety of complicated or longer action steps, biweekly or monthly checkpoints might be the right frequency. Customize your checkpoints so they best address your needs and are appropriate for your specific situation.

> Step 7 Tasks
>
> Look at the plan you've just created, and assess where it makes most sense to build in regular checkpoints for each end goal and milestone. Consider both frequency and timing. Once you've evaluated how often and when your checkpoints should occur, note them on your plan. You can either highlight the day or put in a designation of "CP" on that day.

Key Factors for Success during Stage 4

1. Have Realistic Expectations

Although making change should push you beyond your comfort zone, it is important to remain realistic in your expectations. Setting goals or milestones that are unrealistic or too lofty can set you up for disappointment or potential failure.

Elizabeth had wanted to be a ballerina since she was a young girl, but never pursued her dream. When she turned forty-two, she still yearned for ballet to be part of her life and so made it a goal. Given standards of the profession, it would be unrealistic for Elizabeth to set a goal of becoming a professional ballet dancer at her age. Most ballet professionals reach their prime in their late teens, twenties, and early thirties. As a result, Elizabeth decided not to pursue ballet as a career; she knew that if she did she would likely set herself up for disappointment or failure. Instead, Elizabeth has cho-sen to incorporate ballet into her life by taking classes at a local performing arts school or university. This has made creating and pursuing her goal more realistic.

Another aspect of setting realistic expectations for yourself is that you want to be sure to give yourself enough time to accomplish each step, each milestone, and ultimately each goal. Unrealistic time frames that cause you to rush through any stage of your process could negatively impact your chances of success. Take your time and enjoy the process.

2. KNOW WHAT YOU CAN CONTROL

When creating your plan, your chances of success are highest when you can control your actions and behaviors, and ultimately the outcomes. If, however, you create a plan that is largely dependent on the actions or input of others or on external circumstances, you run the risk of failure. Develop goals, milestones, and action steps that mostly rely on your own abilities so that you have the greatest chance of success.

3. APPEAL TO YOUR EMOTIONAL SIDE

As we've discussed, engaging your emotional side is crucial to the process of personal reinvention and change. Continue to revisit the signs you identified during Stage 1 to recapture the feeling. Also, remind yourself of the strengths, passions, and motivators you identified during Stage 2 so you develop a plan that inspires and encourages you to continue working toward your goals, even during periods of frustration.

4. KEEP THE PLAN SIMPLE

The process that has been outlined throughout this stage has been very detailed. The detail is meant to provide you with a full understanding of how to best navigate and plan for change and personal reinvention. That said, your plan itself should be as simple as possible. If your plan becomes cumbersome or too complicated, take a step back and try to simplify it as best you can. You'll be more likely to stay inspired by simplicity, not complexity.

You now have your plan for personal reinvention. This will guide you throughout the process of reinvention and will help keep you stay on track so you can most effectively reach your goals and see your vision for your best life come to fruition.

Stage 4 Summary

Stage 4 requires that you create a plan to make your vision a reality.

Step 1: Identify Your End goals. Based on your vision, create end goals that follow the SMARTE framework.

Step 2: Research What Is Required. Do research to understand what will be involved to achieve each of your end goals.

Step 3: Prioritize Your Goals. Based on two qualities—impact and difficulty—prioritize your goals so you know what to focus on first, second, third, etc.

Step 4: Break Goals into Milestones and Action Steps. Based on your findings in Step 2, break your end goals into smaller goals—milestones and action steps.

Step 5: Assign Time Frames to Goals and Milestones. Identify appropriate target dates for the completion of each of your milestones and end goals and, if appropriate, action steps.

Step 6: Build In a Rewards System. Identify appropriate rewards that allow you to acknowledge and appreciate your progress as you go through your process.

Step 7: Build In Regular Checkpoints. So that you can properly do the work in Stage 6, identify regular checkpoints at which you will evaluate your progress.

Principle of Change #4
PLANNING FOR CHANGE IS PLANNING TO SUCCEED.

STAGE 5: MAKE IT HAPPEN

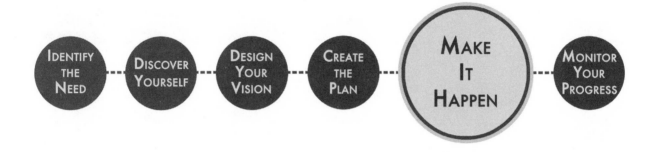

THE ONLY DIFFERENCE BETWEEN SUCCESS AND FAILURE IS THE ABILITY TO TAKE ACTION.

—ALEXANDER GRAHAM BELL

THE PLAN YOU CREATED IN Stage 4 will be your guide throughout your personal reinvention. You should have clear goals and a clear path to follow in order to ultimately help you make your vision a reality. Now, it is time to take your plan and put it into action.

Even the best plans can fail if the execution is faulty. Often, this can be a result of an unforeseen roadblock that seems overwhelmingly difficult to navigate, a lack in dedication or commitment, or a lack in sustained motivation. Regardless, proper action is the precursor to making change successful. This brings us to our fifth Principle of Change:

Principle of Change #5
WITHOUT PROPER ACTION, CHANGE CANNOT OCCUR.

Hopefully, due to all the work you've done thus far, you at least have the initial motivation you need to take the first step. To ensure you have long-term follow-through, however, you'll want to know how to overcome roadblocks when they present themselves, and how to continually fuel your internal motivation and commitment so that you are inspired to constantly make progress.

STAGE 5 ACTION STEPS

STEP 1: FIND THE RIGHT TRACKING TOOL

The first step to execution is to find an effective way to keep track of your progress. You'll want to use a tool that supports you in documenting and tracking your action steps, milestones, and goals. There are a lot of tools you can use, but you want to find the one that you'll be most likely to use and that will most likely work for you.

ROADBLOCK: An Inability to Prioritize Your Own Needs

If you find it difficult to say no to people or to set boundaries with others, you may also find it challenging to prioritize your own needs. Doing so, however, is crucial to your ability to achieve what you want and to accomplishing your goals.

When you can make your needs a priority, you are honoring your commitments to yourself. This allows you to put in the time required to make the changes you want and gives you more control over your life. It builds self-respect and self-confidence, and will actually help you gain the respect and confidence of others as well. To better prioritize your own needs, consider the following:

- **Evaluate Opportunities:** As new opportunities present themselves, evaluate them against your current goals. For instance, if you're asked to work on a special project that will require an extra ten hours per week for several months, no might be the best response if you're trying to spend more time with your family. On the other hand, if you'll be paid overtime, and one of your goals is to buy a house, you may want to consider responding yes so you can put money more quickly toward a down payment.

- **Sweat the Small Stuff:** Our commitments can spiral out of control because we say yes to too many small things. The small things, however, add up. Realize that with every yes you're making a commitment to something that might take you away from your own priorities.

- **Take Your Time:** If you're presented with an opportunity but don't know how to respond, take a day or two to think about it. Rarely is a decision ever so urgent that a response is required immediately. Also, when you take your time to evaluate an opportunity, you are less inclined to respond from an emotional place. Instead, you will be more likely to respond rationally and realistically about what you can and can't commit to.

- **Leave Guilt Behind:** If you don't feel like doing something or know it won't help you toward reaching your own goals, yet you feel obligated, this is a cue that you are doing something out of guilt. In these situations, a no is likely in order. Prioritizing out of guilt prevents us from taking ownership of our lives and our decisions. We instead are letting everybody else's needs come first.

- **Be Up Front and Honest:** Remember, you have every right to prioritize yourself and say no. Whether you're too busy, have more important things to take care of or do, or don't feel an opportunity is something you're genuinely interested in, it's a good reason. Be up front and honest with people so they know where you stand and where your priorities are. This will help them to have a better understanding of what they can and can't expect from you. Try not to waffle or string people along, as this will only prolong the agony.

If, for instance, you avoid technological gadgets or prefer the traditional route of putting pen to paper, then don't choose to put your plan and tracking mechanisms on the computer, an electronic tablet, or any other technological device. Instead, use a device in which you can track your progress by hand—your journal might be ideal. If, however, you sit in front of your computer a good portion of the day or like using technological devices, then you might be better off putting your plan into a software tool like Microsoft Excel or even Microsoft Project. The **End Goals, Milestones, and Action Steps Worksheet** used in Stage 4 is suited for these two programs. There may be other tools or apps you might find helpful; just be sure to use something with which you are most comfortable.

Step 1 Tasks

Regardless of the tool you choose, it should incorporate a reminder of your vision, your big end goals, your milestones, and your action steps, and the respective time frames for each. Further, it should be helpful, not a nuisance. Your tool should be:

- **Supportive of Your Vision:** The tool must support you in living your mission and achieving your vision, goals, milestones, and action steps.

- **Easy to Use:** Your tracking tool should be easy to use so that it helps motivate and encourage you to make progress. Integrate your tool into everyday life so it becomes habitual as opposed to an afterthought.

- **Matched to You:** Your tool should match your personality, your needs, and how you function as an individual. If you find using or updating a tool to be a hassle, it may actually undermine your efforts.

- **Portable:** In order to update your progress easily and regularly, regardless of where you are or what you're doing, the tool you choose should be portable so you can bring it wherever you want.

STEP 2: BUILD IN TIME REQUIRED

Making time to achieve your goals and follow your path is a must for success. Change is going to take some effort, and it will require commitment and dedication. Build in the time you need, to make sure you don't short-change your vision and plan.

Step 2 Tasks

A few ideas to ensure you build sufficient time into your process:

- **Schedule It:** If you use a personal calendar or scheduling device, block off a specific time each day or week to dedicate to your plan. We are more likely to commit to our action items if we build them into our schedule.

- **Reprioritize:** If your days or weeks are packed with commitments and you don't feel that you have time to dedicate to your goals, then it means reprioritization might be in order. Evaluate your current priorities and obligations and assess what you can cut out or put on hold. When making decisions and prioritizing activities, it pays to weigh options around your values and your vision. If an activity or an option does not support you in meeting your goals, it should not be a high priority.

- **Inform Others:** Let people who may be impacted by your new priorities know you need more time for yourself. If you are open about your needs, they'll be more likely to respect them. If they aren't respectful, set clear boundaries to ensure they don't eat into the time you need.

- **Reduce Time Wasters:** We often fall victim to spending a lot of time doing unimportant activities. Although many of these activities provide a source of entertainment, they take up a lot of time we could be spending on more important and meaningful things, especially when time is tight. For instance, time spent watching television, playing video games, or reading through Facebook and Twitter posts could be put to better use. If finding time for your goals is difficult, try cutting back on these more frivolous activities. Even a half hour less of television per day can add up, making a big difference.

STEP 3: REMOVE NEGATIVE OBSTACLES

Our past negative experiences can cause us to think that we can't do things when in actuality we can. This kind of thinking can be one of our biggest saboteurs, undermining our ability to make change.

Looking back at the work you did in **Stage 2: Discover Yourself**, you should have a good sense of the obstacles you faced in your past, and what familial or life experiences caused you to shy away from challenges or from taking risks. If these obstacles still exist in your current life, it pays to find ways to remove them.

Step 3 Tasks

Negativity can come from several sources. To minimize negative obstacles in your life, consider the following ideas:

1. **Deal with Unhealthy Relationships:** If there are individuals in your life who tear you down or don't support you, your vision, or your goals, they may undermine your ability to achieve what you want. If this is an issue, try to minimize your exposure to these people, or avoid them altogether. A few things that might help:

- **Minimize Toxic Relationships:** Toxic relationships often come hand in hand with negativity. If an individual makes you feel bad about yourself, what you do, or how you are, then the person is toxic. Toxic people often make others feel bad so that they can feel better about themselves. You can try to speak to the individual about how you feel, but doing so may not produce the results you want. She may dismiss you or slough off your message. If these individuals are family members or work colleagues, it can be especially difficult to completely remove them from your life. In these cases, fill your time with healthier and more supportive relationships, which will naturally reduce the time you are able to spend with those who are toxic.

- **Set Clear Boundaries:** Set boundaries with the negative people in your life. If they cross a line and go too far with their personal commentary or opinions, let them know that although you love and care for them, their negativity isn't welcome. Explain to them that if they can't be positive or respectful, then you will need to minimize your time with them.

- **Find Positive People:** The more you surround yourself with positive, happy, energetic people the less room you have for those who are negative. Further, there is a contagiousness that we get from being around people who are living the way we want to live or acting the way we want to act. Their confidence and happiness, as well as their positive habits, rub off on us.

2. **Avoid Unhealthy Environments:** The environments in which we live, work, and play can have a tremendous impact on our ability to make change. When we are in environments that are stressful, challenging, or difficult, change becomes less likely. This can include where we work, where we live, and even where we choose to spend our leisure time. In *Switch: How to Change Things When Change Is Hard*, Chip and Dan Heath talk about shaping the path to make change less difficult. They urge you to separate yourself from the environment that cues old, unhealthy habits, and instead put yourself in an environment that supports, and is most appropriate for, the changes you want to make. If you find that certain situations or environments bring out bad habits or cause you to feel negative, lack confidence, or act out of congruence with your values, vision, or mission, you may want to consider avoiding them altogether—or at the very least, minimize your exposure to them as much as possible.

3. **Deal with Negativity from Within:** Our barriers to change may not always come from external sources. They can often come from within ourselves.

- **Address Fear:** Many of us let fear and anxiety impair our ability to move forward and achieve the things that will bring happiness into our lives. If you find that fear is hindering your capacity to progress in your plan, focus on the things you want to do and imagine yourself doing them. Push out the fear, and instead imagine the positive feelings and happiness you'll experience. Reread the stories you were asked to write about overcoming fear during **Stage 2: Discover Yourself**. Apply the same methodology now and ask yourself the following questions:

  o What are you afraid of?

  o What do you feel?

o   Is your fear based in reality?

o   Are you in control?

Use your **New You Journal** to write the story. Think of the best-case scenario of what would happen if you were to take the risk and push your fears aside. Reread this story whenever you feel overwhelmed by your fears.

- **Turn "I Can't" into "I Can":** Positive thoughts beget positive results. The more we think we can do something, the more we will be able to do it. On the other hand, if we continually tell ourselves we can't do something, we limit ourselves, and it becomes a self-fulfilling prophecy. Negative thinking actually paralyzes us and prevents us from making the changes we want. Remind yourself to maintain a growth mindset. Stay positive and have a can-do attitude. The more positive you are and the more you believe in your abilities, the more positive things will come your way and the more capable you'll be.

Step 4: Develop Your Support Network

Although you are personally responsible for your reinvention and accomplishments, building a support network to help you "cross the finish line" can be beneficial too. Further, when we inform others of our intentions, it gives us a stronger sense of accountability. Think about your milestones and goals, and identify areas in which you may need to solicit help. Look to friends, family members, or even experts to guide you through some of the action steps you need to take to reach your final destination.

Step 4 Tasks

There are two ways your support network can be helpful: emotionally and professionally. Family members and friends will most likely provide emotional support. Essentially, they act as your "cheering section." Those individuals who will be best at supporting you will:

- Understand your values, mission, and purpose in going through a personal reinvention

- Have your best interests at heart, regardless of their own opinions

- Remain objective and nonjudgmental

- Add to your process, not take away from it

- Be someone you can trust and confide in

- Be thoughtful in providing you with insights, feedback, and opinions

Professionals will most likely be supportive by providing their expertise and knowledge in educating you in areas you may not be familiar with. They may even help support you in reaching your goals faster. For instance, if one of your goals is to become fit and you decide as part of the process you want to train for a marathon, you might want to hire a running coach or consult with a fitness nutrit. If you are seriously considering a career change, you might want to consider working with a career coach or life coach. If you are trying to reinvent within the social or emotional dimension of well-being, you may benefit from working with a psychologist, psychiatrist, social worker, or life coach as well. Professionals who will be best at supporting you will:

- Provide expertise and support that is relevant to the changes you want to make

- Be legitimate experts in their field

- Come highly recommended by others who have used their services

- Remain professional, yet sympathetic

- Support you throughout the process while pushing you to go beyond your comfort zone

- Be honest about your progress and what you could be doing better

Ultimately, cultivating a support network should help guide and encourage you as you work toward achieving your goals. If you find that it doesn't, you may want to rethink the people you've chosen to be a part of your network.

ROADBLOCK: Naysayers and Reinvention Saboteurs

Although sharing your vision for a personal reinvention with others can be helpful, it can also be a hindrance if those individuals are not supportive. If they undermine you or are pessimistic, they will likely have a negative impact on you and your efforts. Look for individuals who fit the criteria outlined in **Step 4: Develop Your Support Network** when choosing to share your goals and intentions with others.

Step 5: Create Your Motivational Toolbox

By now you should have developed a plan that inspires you. At the same time, it is only realistic that there may be times when you could use a little extra help in keeping your motivation levels high. Creating a personal motivational toolbox will provide you with tools that appeal to your emotional side, and encourage and inspire you when you feel less than excited about the changes you want to make.

Step 5 Tasks

Your motivational toolbox should inspire you, especially when you need it most. The following ideas are popular with many individuals, but feel free to tap into what you've identified as your personal motivators from Stage 2, and incorporate components or activities that speak to them directly.

1. **Personal Affirmations:** Although affirmations may sound hokey, they're actually very useful in cultivating a positive outlook and a can-do attitude. Use affirmations in a genuine and

thoughtful way to reprogram your mind and push past negative thoughts so they become more positive and encouraging. According to Stephen R. Covey, author of *The 7 Habits of Highly Effective People*, a good affirmation will be personal to you and your vision. It will be positive, in the present tense, and emotionally inspiring. It should also be visual, meaning that you should be able to visualize it either by writing it somewhere so you can see it on a daily basis or by picturing it in your mind. A few examples of affirmations:

- I am smart and successful in everything I do.

- I am capable of achieving what I want.

- I make healthy choices in the foods I eat, and I exercise regularly so that I can be the healthiest possible.

- I deserve love and happiness.

Using the **List of Affirmations Worksheet** in **Part III: The New You Journal** as a template, write down affirmations you believe will be relevant, positive, and helpful to you and your attempts to achieve your vision and end goals. Read them in the morning; read them at night; read them out loud to yourself at any time you feel you could use a little extra encouragement.

2. **Ask Yourself a Question:** Although affirmations work for many, asking yourself a simple question might actually provide you with more motivation. In "Will We Succeed? The Science of Self-Motivation," an article published in *ScienceDaily* in 2010, Professor Dolores Albarracin of University of Illinois explains that individuals who *ask* themselves if they will perform a task generally do better than those who *tell* themselves that they will. Albarracin's team believes that by asking yourself a question, you are more likely to build your own motivation. For instance:

- Will I make healthy choices today?

- Will I go to the gym today?

- Will I be open and trusting today?

- Can I let go of past hurts or resentments?

- Will I find my dream job today?

- Will I live in the moment today?

- Will I have a positive outlook today?

Come up with questions that are specific to your plan, milestones, and goals. Ask them of yourself each day to increase your motivation levels.

3. **Fake It Until You Make It:** See yourself as the changed person you want to be. The more you think of yourself in a certain way, the more you will *be* a certain way. Further, if you don't feel motivated, you might find faking it to be helpful too. Studies show that when we don't feel a certain way (e.g., confident, motivated, etc.) but visualize ourselves or act as if we do, we can actually cause ourselves to be or feel that way over time.

4. **Don't Be Hard on Yourself:** If things don't go as planned or you find yourself missing target dates within your plan, don't be too hard on yourself. This promotes negative thinking. Instead, try to stay light and positive.

5. **Revisit Your Accomplishments:** You identified your accomplishments in **Stage 2: Discover Yourself**. When you feel discouraged or find that completing tasks is especially difficult, revisit the work you completed on the **My Accomplishments Worksheet**. Read through the steps you took and the obstacles you overcame to successfully achieve your goals. You might even want to display reminders of them in highly visible places so they are constantly at the top of your mind.

6. **Don't Forget the Rewards:** Finally, be sure to implement the rewards you built into your plan, and reward yourself when you reach your milestones and achieve your end goals. Although your rewards shouldn't be the primary driver for change, they are an important part of your plan, because they promote acknowledgment and appreciation for the work and effort you put into your goals.

STEP 6: MODIFY KEY HABIT LOOPS THAT REQUIRE CHANGE

In *The Power of Habit: Why We Do What We Do in Life and Business*, Charles Duhigg tell us that in order for us to make permanent, long-lasting change, we need to examine our current "habit loops" and modify them to develop new, healthier habits that support the change.

Duhigg explains that the habit loop is made up of the following three components:

- **Cue:** The signal that causes you to do the habit in the first place.

- **Routine:** The action you take that ultimately leads to a reward.

- **Reward:** What you receive that is pleasurable from the routine.

In order to modify your habits or behaviors, Duhigg suggests that you find which part of the loop is causing unfavorable results. Modifying that part will create healthier habits.

> *Suzanne is a type 2 diabetic who was at risk for heart disease. After her doctors increased her medication dose for a third time, Suzanne asked if there was anything she should be doing to decrease her reliance on medicine. Her doctors told her that if she lost weight and modified certain behaviors and habits, there would be a chance that she could reduce her dependence on medication. As a result, Suzanne was inspired to undergo a personal reinvention around her physical well-being. She wanted to lose weight, decrease her dependency on her medicine, and reduce her risks for heart disease.*
>
> *Since she began a new job six months prior to the doctor's visit, Suzanne had gained about fifteen pounds. Given the recent increase in her medication, she couldn't help but wonder if the added weight was contributing to this increased reliance. After spending some time considering possible causes, she identified a new habit she had developed since starting the job. Every Friday, she and her colleagues would go out to a local bar after work. She would enjoy two or three cocktails, and over the course of the evening, the group would generally order several appetizers to share. By no means were the appetizers healthy; they were often fried, high-calorie foods.*
>
> *Although Suzanne enjoyed the ritual of going out with her colleagues, she was also aware that a good portion of her weight gain was possibly due to the extra calories she was consuming each Friday night. As a result, she thought this habit might be worth modifying.*

She first identified the cue, the routine, and the reward:

- **Cue:** *When work was over on Friday afternoons*

- **Routine:** *Going to a local bar and ordering cocktails, and eating unhealthy food*

- **Reward:** *Relaxation, socialization, and celebrating the end of the workweek*

Realizing the cue couldn't change (Friday afternoons would remain Friday afternoons) and that the reward wasn't unhealthy (it was about socialization, not the alcohol or food itself), Suzanne realized she had an opportunity to modify an unhealthy habit. Specifically, she needed to change the routine. To do so, Suzanne did two things: (1) she brought a healthy, filling snack with her each Friday; right before going out to the pub, she would eat the snack so she wouldn't be hungry at the pub; and (2) instead of ordering an alcoholic beverage, Suzanne started ordering club soda and lime. As a result, the modified loop looked like this:

- **Cue:** *When work was over on Friday afternoons*

- **Routine:** *Eating a healthy, filling snack before going to the local pub and ordering a club soda and lime to drink*

- **Reward:** *Relaxation, socialization, and celebrating the end of the workweek*

In only a month, Suzanne was able to lose about ten pounds and was thrilled to find that she could still enjoy the socialization with her colleagues without the added weight. Inspired by this one change, Suzanne learned to modify other habit loops that were contributing to her poorer health, and after six months she managed to reduce almost all her medications.

As you go through your plan for personal reinvention, you will most likely identify habits that need to change. Use the habit loop as a way to modify unhealthy habits so they become healthier and more supportive of your overall vision and end goals.

Step 6 Tasks

The habits you need to change may not be immediately noticeable. As you go through the steps of your plan, pay close attention to your current habits. Be mindful of those that are unhealthy, producing unwanted results, or are counteracting your ability to change. For each habit you identify as needing modification, use the **Duhigg's Habit Loop Modification Worksheet** in **Part III: The New You Journal** as a template to complete the following tasks:

1. **Identify the Cue, Routine, and Reward:** Examine the habit and identify the cue, routine, and reward. Write each component in its respective place in the section titled "Current Habit Loop":

- **Cue:** The signal that causes you to do the habit in the first place

- **Routine:** The action you take that will ultimately give you a reward

- **Reward:** The pleasurable result. What is the end goal? What pleasurable experience do you get out of it?

2. **Decide Which Part Needs to Change:** Decide what part of the habit loop needs to be modified. Specifically, what part of the habit loop is causing unhealthy or unwanted results? In the section titled "What Needs to Change," write in which part of the habit loop should be modified.

3. **Identify Opportunities for Modification:** Once you understand which part of the habit loop needs to change, come up with ways to modify it so you can reap healthier or more attractive results or outcomes. Write these in the section titled "Opportunities for Modification." Refer to the example of Suzanne for a breakdown of what this might look like.

4. **Rewrite the Loop:** Finally, in the section titled "The New Habit Loop," write in the new components of the loop you just created.

STEP 7: ADDRESS INCONSISTENT BEHAVIOR

For change to stick, it needs to become your standard way of operating. It needs to become part of who you are. If you only maintain change on a superficial level, when it is convenient or when it is easy, then the change you are hoping to make won't stick or become standard protocol within your life. This is called *inconsistent behavior*.

In *Switch: How to Change Things When Change Is Hard*, the Heath brothers use the term "bright spots" to describe moments when things are working for certain groups or individuals even though they aren't for others. You can apply this thinking to you and your own actions. If there are certain times or situations in which your desired behaviors are consistent, then you should look for ways to replicate them. If there are times, however, when your desired behaviors aren't consistent, you know to avoid those scenarios.

> *Kristi decided that one of her goals was to practice and play the piano more regularly so that she could perform in a local concert. Music brought her great happiness, but she always felt she never had the time to play. Kristi had a full-time job, so practicing during the week was difficult. Using the concert as a motivator, she decided she would try playing at night after work or in the morning before work.*

> *After a couple of months, Kristi realized she wasn't getting better. Her concert was only a month away, and she needed to find a way to improve. In looking at her schedule over the previous couple of months, she noticed that when she put practice off until the evening, she was inconsistent. She often had reasons she couldn't practice: she would have to work late, she was tired, she had business dinners, her colleagues would want to go out after work, and so on. As a result, she played only about 30 to 40 percent of the time when she scheduled her practice for the evenings. However, when Kristi decided she would play in the morning, she did so 100 percent of the time. Not only was her practice in the morning productive, but she also found that it put her in great spirits for the rest of the day. Kristi decided that in order to properly prepare for the recital, she needed to commit to playing solely in the morning. Her morning practice was her "bright spot" or "moment of consistency."*

> *When Kristi changed her schedule to morning practices 100 percent of the time, she saw great progress in her performance. Her hands became more agile, and she was able to play at much faster tempos. She also found that she could play more challenging music. Moreover, she went from practicing two or three times a week to five or six after the schedule adjustment.*

When the day of the recital arrived, Kristi was ready and excited. The performance went brilliantly, earning her a standing ovation.

Kristi discovered her "moment of consistency" so that she could transform inconsistent behavior to behavior that was more reliable. This helped her to successfully reach her goal.

To address your own inconsistencies, you'll want to understand what changes you've successfully made and why so you can learn from them. You'll also want to identify the changes you are struggling with and analyze if there is anything you can apply to make your behaviors more consistent.

Step 7 Tasks

To help solidify changes and create more permanent habits that are positive, use the **Inconsistent Behaviors Worksheet** in **Part III: The New You Journal** as a template to document your answers:

1. **Document Results of Change:** Every time you successfully make a change, document how your changes are positively impacting your life by answering the following questions in the section titled "Results of Change" within the **Inconsistent Behaviors Worksheet:**

   - What changes have I successfully made?

   - How do these changes make me feel?

   - How do I feel about the progress I've made thus far?

   - How would I feel if I stopped this change or habit?

2. **Identify Inconsistencies:** As you progress through your plan, identify changes you struggle with and the behaviors that continue to be inconsistent in the section titled "Inconsistencies." Answer the following questions:

   - What behaviors are inconsistent?

- How do I feel when I'm inconsistent?

- How has this affected my ability to move forward?

3. **Find Your Moments of Consistency:** In looking at the behaviors you identified in Task 2, identify any moments when your behaviors were favorable. Use the section titled "Moments of Consistency" in the **Inconsistent Behaviors Worksheet** template to answer the following questions:

- Have there been times when I've successfully engaged in behaviors that support or work toward the change?

- What were the "moments of consistency" I might be able to apply?

- How can I change my circumstances or environment to help me in creating more consistent behavior?

If you feel your changes begin to slip, revisit Tasks 1–3. What you document under "Results of Change" should act as a reminder of the benefits you feel when you successfully make change, motivating you to stay the course. The behaviors documented under "Inconsistencies" should tell you what behaviors need to be modified so they are more consistent; and finally, the "Moments of Consistency" you identify should help you in making less consistent behaviors more so.

STEP 8: EXPECT TO FAIL...A LITTLE

Change is a process, and a messy one at that. Although maintaining a positive attitude throughout your reinvention is crucial to your success, understanding that failure is inevitable and a natural part of the process is too.

When we expect to fail, it makes the actual act of failing much less painful or discouraging. It allows us to accept it, learn from it, and move on much more easily than if we expect everything will work out as we plan the first time. Planning to fail is consistent with the growth mindset discussed in Carol Dweck's *Mindset: The New*

Psychology of Success. It gives us permission to make mistakes, to struggle a bit, to fall off the horse—all with the intention of making us stronger and more successful in the end.

As you go through your plan for personal reinvention, have a slight expectation that failure will happen. If it does, embrace it as part of the process. If it doesn't, well, then you'll be pleasantly surprised.

Step 8 Tasks

If at any point during your process you run up against failure, use the **My Failures of Reinvention Worksheet** in **Part III: The New You Journal** as a template to do the following:

1. In the column labeled "Failures," list the failure you experience.

2. In the column labeled "Causes," describe why you think failure occurred. Was it a result of your plan's design? Was it a result of circumstances that were out of your control?

3. In the column labeled "Lessons Learned," describe what you took away from the experience. Did it provide you with further clarity? Did it help you to see a more efficient or effective way of doing things? Did it give you better understanding of yourself?

4. In the last column, "Moving Forward," discuss how the failure can be used to help you move forward with your plan. Think about ways in which you can apply what you've learned to improve upon your plan or in how you approach change.

KEY FACTORS FOR SUCCESS DURING STAGE 5

1. ACCOUNTABILITY

Accountability requires you to take ownership of your actions. There will always be conditions or situations that you can't control. You do, however, have control over how you choose to handle them.

Your life is a result of your decisions, thoughts, and behaviors, not your circumstances. Understanding and believing this puts you in the driver's seat of your life, and gives you the power to achieve what you want. Instead of waiting for things to happen, you make them happen. To be accountable, avoid blaming other people, conditions, or past experiences for what happens today and in your future. Instead, recognize that you have the power to succeed, to create your optimal life, and to attain the happiness you desire.

Build Self-Confidence for Change That Sticks

Self-confidence is extremely important in our ability to achieve our goals and create the life we desire. It can, however, be one of the most difficult attributes to develop. Whether we are burdened with painful childhood memories, unhealthy relationships that beat us down emotionally, or insecurities as a result of societal pressures, self-confidence can seem highly unattainable. The truth is, self-confidence is challenging for all of us...even for those of us who appear extremely confident, pulled together, and self-assured. The good news is that self-confidence can be cultivated, and the more you do so, the more of it you'll have. Here are a few tips to develop yours:

- **Build It from Within:** In building self-confidence it is imperative that you look to do so from within. There will always be people who don't approve of us or like us, and so seeking their approval is self-defeating and a waste of energy. We never fully achieve the self-confidence we really want. Find your confidence through how you view yourself. Remind yourself of your strengths, your accomplishments, and the positive qualities you possess, and all that you should be proud of.

- **Stay Positive:** Individuals with a glass-half-full mentality tend to be happier, more confident, and more comfortable with themselves. They manage stress better and are more likely to persevere and push through difficult situations and circumstances. Also, positive people are more willing to take risks and conquer their fears, making them more likely to perform well, achieve their goals, and be successful. Setbacks are merely viewed as minor and are easily overcome. Negativity, on the other hand, eats away at self-confidence and keeps us in an immobile place. When you start to think negatively about yourself, a situation or another person, stop and instead find something positive on which to focus.

- **Take Care of Yourself:** Studies show that taking pride in yourself has a tremendous impact on your confidence. The more you value and respect your health, your body, and even your appearance, the better you will feel. Take time to take care of yourself and your overall well-being.

- **Make Eye Contact:** Making eye contact can be challenging, but the more you do it, the easier it will become. It sends others a message that you are comfortable connecting with them. In turn, they feel more comfortable and confident around you, making dialogue and time with them easy and effortless. This ease with which you interact with others will help boost your own self-confidence.

- **Be Complimentary:** When we find fault with others it is often because we find fault with ourselves. Finding the good in others, however, allows you to see the good in yourself.

- **Smile:** Although there may be times when we aren't in the mood to smile, forcing a smile can help you break through some of the uneasiest of times. Further, smiling at others often elicits a smile back, sending positive vibes your way.

2. PASSION

In **Stage 1: Identify the Need**, we discussed the first Principle of Change: Discontent + passion drive change. In truth, passion needs to be a part of the whole process of reinvention for you to be successful. Passion stems from your emotional side and is instrumental to staying motivated and inspired. If at any time you don't feel passionate about what you are doing or where you are going, it could be an indication that something isn't right and needs to be addressed or adjusted. At these times, think about why you aren't passionate and figure out what needs to change in order for the passion to be refueled.

3. DEDICATION AND DETERMINATION

As exciting as it will be to embark on the positive changes you will make, it is important to be cognizant of the work, energy, and time it will take. Consistent dedication and determination is crucial to your ability to achieve what you want. Be ready to do the work you need to do, to roll up your sleeves, to get dirty and messy, and to throw yourself at full throttle into the effort.

If you are working toward multiple goals, you may find that the process seems complex at times, and possibly even daunting. When this happens, take a step back and try to remember the bigger picture of your vision and your end goals. Also, be sure to use some of the tools from your motivational toolbox for inspiration. That is why you created it.

4. THE FOUR SELVES

Without you and your own actions, change cannot happen. You, and only you, are instrumental to creating the life you want. With this in mind, there are four factors that are key to your success, and each one specifically pertains to you and your "selves": self-leadership, self-management, self-empowerment, and self-confidence.

1. **Self-Leadership:** Leadership in its traditional form means having a vision and successfully motivating and inspiring others to follow you in accomplishing that vision. Self-leadership requires that you do this for yourself. You need to define your vision for the future, align yourself and your actions behind it, and

inspire yourself to make it happen, even in the face of uncertainty or as obstacles present themselves. This is a never-ending practice. There may be times when you are not motivated, but the leader within you will need to find a way to reinvigorate your passion and inspire you to continue.

2. **Self-Management:** Self-leadership is important in creating your vision and inspiring you to make the change, but self-management is what ensures that you follow through with the plan and do the work you need to do to make it happen. It requires diligence, and that you organize your life and your actions around your vision. Self-management keeps you on track so you can follow through on action steps, meet milestones, and eventually achieve your goals.

3. **Self-Empowerment:** Self-empowerment is what helps you to overcome negativity and the "I can't" mentality, and instead, gives you an "I can" attitude. To truly feel empowered, you'll need to arm yourself with all that is required to succeed, including learning new skills or gaining new knowledge. If you feel as though you don't have the right tools to accomplish your goals, stay out of an "I can't" or "but" attitude, and instead adopt one of "How can I?" Go back to school, get experience and practice, solicit help from professionals, and do what you need to do to become the person you want to be. Remember, constant change and learning means continual growth. This keeps you from becoming stagnant and allows you to challenge yourself so that you can be the best that you can be.

4. **Self-Confidence:** Self-confidence enables a deeper belief in yourself, helping you to forge ahead, even when things seem uncertain. It allows you to overcome fears and challenges more easily, while maintaining a positive attitude. Also, studies show the more confident you are, the higher your chances of success. Luckily, self-confidence builds on itself: as you continue to achieve, your self-confidence continues to grow. This will make taking on risks and challenges easier and easier.

Stage 5 Summary

Stage 5 is focused on developing tools and the infrastructure you need to follow through on the plan you created in Stage 4.

Step 1: Find the Right Tracking Tool. Choose a tracking tool that will help you keep track of your progress throughout your personal reinvention.

Step 2: Build In Time Required. Ensure that you make time for the changes you want to make and the goals you want to achieve.

Step 3: Remove Negative Obstacles. Find ways to remove obstacles that present themselves along your path. This pertains to negative or unhealthy relationships and environments, or even negativity within yourself.

Step 4: Develop Your Support Network. Lean on friends and family for emotional support, and utilize experts for help and assistance in achieving your goals and vision.

Step 5: Create Your Motivational Toolbox. Develop a personalized toolbox of motivational tools that will continue to inspire you along your path to personal reinvention.

Step 6: Modify Key Habit Loops That Require Change. Modify habits that are obstacles to change or that are producing unhealthy results.

Step 7: Address Inconsistent Behavior. Identify when you are best able to maintain specific healthy and productive behaviors and find ways to encourage consistency.

Step 8: Expect to Fail…A Little. Set the expectation that failure is a healthy and necessary part of the process of change.

Principle of Change #5
WITHOUT PROPER ACTION, CHANGE CANNOT OCCUR.

STAGE 6: MONITOR YOUR PROGRESS

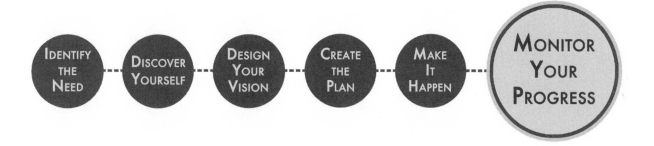

VICTORY BELONGS TO THE MOST PERSEVERING.

—NAPOLÉON BONAPARTE

CREATING YOUR BEST LIFE IS a process—one that needs to be nurtured and reevaluated on an ongoing basis. As you proceed on your path to personal reinvention, monitoring how you are doing will be instrumental to your success.

Regularly monitoring your progress provides numerous benefits. For starters, it keeps you abreast of the positive impacts your changes are making in your life. This will continue to motivate you in making further change. Second, by monitoring your progress, you continue to hold yourself accountable for the results (or lack of results) you see. Finally, it can strengthen your plan for change by giving you an opportunity to evaluate what is working and what isn't so that you can make appropriate modifications in a timely manner. You may find your original plan needs to be adjusted to accommodate changes you make or new circumstances that arise. Or, you may find your action steps or milestones aren't working as well as you had hoped, and thus they need to be modified. Essentially, change often brings about more change, and as a result, plans need to evolve accordingly. This brings us to our sixth and final Principle of Change:

Principle of Change #6
CHANGE IS AN EVER-EVOLVING PROCESS.

STAGE 6 ACTION STEPS

There are few steps required during Stage 6. It is still important, however, to the process. Essentially, it requires that you evaluate your plan for its effectiveness and to see if it is working, and to modify it as you see fit. Without this step you run the risk of continuing on a path that is unproductive, which could ultimately cause you to stagnate. Or, you may continue on the wrong path, which could take you further away from your vision and achieving your goals.

STEP 1: EVALUATE AT EACH CHECKPOINT

At each checkpoint you identified in **Stage 4: Create the Plan**, you will want to briefly analyze how you are progressing and evaluate if you are on the right track.

Step 1 Tasks

Use the **Checkpoint Evaluation Worksheet** in **Part III: The New You Journal** as a template to respond to the following tasks:

1. Based on your responses to the following questions, place a checkmark in either the "Yes" or "No" column of the worksheet:

   - Am I making progress toward the upcoming milestone or goal?

   - Am I staying true to my vision, values, and mission statement?

   - Do I feel comfortable with and in control of my current action steps?

   - Do they feel realistic?

   - Am I motivated to continue forward?

   - Is everything working well in the plan?

2. Provide qualitative feedback about your plan and the process you are going through in the section titled "How It's Going." Discuss how you feel about your progress, your accomplishments, and any setbacks or other issues you've had along the way. Also, provide any insights you've gained from going through the plan you developed.

If you answered no to any of the questions in the checklist or expressed any concerns in the qualitative section of the evaluation, you should consider making modifications to your plan.

STEP 2: REVISE AS NECESSARY

Based on your answers from Step 1, you will now modify your end goals, milestones, or action steps to address anything that isn't working optimally.

Step 2 Tasks

1. Think about what you can do to change your current plan to make it better. Ask yourself:

    - How do I better align my goals, milestones, and action steps with my vision, values, and mission statement?

    - How do I adjust my plan so I'm more comfortable with it or it is more effective?

    - What can I do to make my plan more realistic?

    - How might I boost my motivation? Are there any other tools I can create for my toolbox?

2. Evaluate if any of your habit loops need modification, and if so, apply what you learned in **Step 6: Modify Key Habit Loops That Require Change** in Stage 5.

3. Evaluate whether your behaviors and changes have been consistent. If not, identify relevant moments of consistency that might be helpful. Apply what you learned in **Step 7: Address Inconsistent Behavior** in Stage 5.

4. Use the information you uncovered in Tasks 1–3 to revise your **End Goals, Milestones, and Action Steps Worksheet**. If you are using a separate tracking tool, reflect the changes you make to the worksheet there as well.

Remember that revising your plan doesn't mean you've failed or that you should feel bad about your progress. As we discussed in **Step 8: Expect to Fail...A Little** in Stage 5, it is all part of the process. Keep a positive can-do attitude as you make revisions, and try to see your modifications as a way to make your plan more effective and to reignite your passion.

Step 3: Repeat on a Regular Basis

Continue to monitor your progress at every checkpoint. If changes are required, be sure to modify your plan so that it adheres to all that you've learned throughout the book. Your plan should contain all the components outlined in **Stage 4: Create the Plan**, and your follow-through should be consistent with **Stage 5: Make It Happen**.

Key Factors for Success during Stage 6

1. Flexibility

It is important to remain flexible as you monitor your progress. If you find that parts of your original plan aren't working, it is essential that you remain objective about what didn't work, and let go of the disappointment so you can improve upon it. This will enable you to learn from the experience and adjust things so they work better in the future. To maintain flexibility, consider the following tips:

- **Allow for Gray Areas:** The process of change has a number of gray areas in it. It is never black or white, right or wrong. There are countless ways a situation can be handled or ways things can be done.

- **Accept and Move Forward:** If it turns out you think you could have designed a better plan, accept the outcome and move forward. Don't get stuck in the past or get angry with yourself; neither of these are productive behaviors. As discussed, failure and mistakes are often wonderful tools in ultimately achieving success.

- **Stay Positive:** Instead of focusing on the fact that a part of the plan isn't working, focus on how you handle the situation. Maintain a positive attitude, as it will have a much bigger impact on the overall outcome of the situation than the mistake or wrong turn made.

- **Learn from Mistakes:** Always look for opportunities to learn from decisions you feel weren't in your best interest. This will teach you how to better deal with things in the future and make you better prepared.

ROADBLOCK: STUBBORNNESS

It is very easy to become attached to your plan for reinvention. After all, you've put a lot of time and effort into developing it. Unfortunately, this can also make it difficult to let go of what isn't working.

Stubbornness hinders us from making progress, because we waste time with ineffective activities. We end up running in place, going nowhere—or worse, we may find ourselves going backward. This can be frustrating and ultimately may cause us to give up altogether. Disallow stubbornness to set, by using the following tips:

1. **Take Yourself Out of the Situation:** We tend to be good at seeing the reality in other people's situations, but not so much for ourselves. Instead of thinking about this as your own plan, pretend the plan is a friend's and you are advising him (with his solicitation, of course) on how to make it better. If you were to give advice on ways to improve it, what would you tell him? How would you see the situation? What changes would you recommend? What could he do to be more successful?

2. **Think about the Big Picture:** When we get caught up in the details of a plan, it limits our ability to see the bigger picture. Remind yourself of why you have embarked on change in the first place. Revisit your values, your vision, and your mission statement so you can focus on the overall picture instead.

3. **Remove the Emotion:** The reason many of us tend to get stuck in a rut of following through with plans that don't work is that we become emotionally attached. Look at your plan objectively and detach yourself from it emotionally. Eliminate feelings of negativity or criticism, and instead stay in an analytical frame of mind by focusing on how you can make the situation or plan better.

4. **Feel the Benefits:** If you modify your original plan, it is because you are inevitably looking to succeed in the end. Imagine how it would feel if you achieve your goals. Imagine how it would feel if you could achieve them more effectively and quickly. Associate the revisions you make with these feelings of potential accomplishment and efficiency. Stubbornness and an inability to admit a need for necessary changes to your plan will only hinder your ability to succeed. Stay flexible and open to the evolution you have to go through to make change work.

2. Patience

As much as we'd like change to happen overnight, it will take time. If you give up or stop before you are completely done going through your plan and all your changes, you may fall short of reaching your goals, lose momentum, or potentially revert back to past habits or behaviors.

If we make our goals or milestones too big, we can become frustrated or impatient or lose motivation to continue on with more difficult changes. Making smaller changes helps us to feel as though we are making progress and accomplishing along the way. To encourage patience, consider the following:

1. **Make Changes as Small as Necessary:** As mentioned, there is no big change that doesn't require many smaller changes. If you feel frustrated with how long it is taking to successfully make a change or reach a goal, it might mean that your changes or goals are too big. Reevaluate your current milestones and goals and see if you can make them smaller. Smaller milestones may bring a feeling of accomplishment on a more frequent basis.

2. **Celebrate Your Accomplishments:** As we discussed in **Stage 4: Create the Plan**, building a rewards system into your plan will help keep your motivation levels high. It will also do wonders for your patience. When you regularly acknowledge and appreciate your efforts, it makes it easier to wait for longer-term benefits and accomplishments to come to fruition.

3. Perseverance

"If at first you don't succeed, try, try again." Success requires resilience and perseverance that get you through the unexpected ups and downs of the process. When things seem difficult or don't seem to be working, these qualities are especially important. Keep looking for ways to make your plan better and more effective or efficient. Learn from mistakes and from what didn't work so you don't repeat those mistakes or decisions again in the future. Maintain a positive, can-do attitude and believe in yourself at all times.

Stage 6 Summary

Stage 6 requires you to monitor your progress at key checkpoints and throughout your personal reinvention.

Step 1: Evaluate at Each Checkpoint. At each checkpoint, evaluate your progress. Look for opportunities to improve your plan so you can be more effective in achieving your goals.

Step 2: Revise as Necessary. Revise your plan to respond to your findings from Step 1. Also, look at your habits to see if there are any habit loops that should be modified or inconsistent behaviors that need to be addressed.

Step 3: Repeat on a Regular Basis. Throughout your plan, continually monitor your progress.

Principle of Change #6
CHANGE IS AN EVER-EVOLVING PROCESS.

A Final Word

You now have all the tools and information you need to make change, to embark on a personal reinvention, and to be your best. You learned about all the stages important to your path to personal reinvention and how they will help you be successful in achieving the life you want. The path and its stages are based on six important Principles of Change:

#1: Discontent + passion drive change.
#2: Self-awareness is the foundation for change.
#3: Vision gives change meaningful direction.
#4: Planning for change is planning to succeed.
#5: Without proper action, change cannot occur.
#6: Change is an ever-evolving process.

In **Stage 1: Identify the Need**, you learned how to identify rational, physical, and emotional signs signaling a change or reinvention might be of benefit. In **Stage 2: Discover Yourself**, you learned the importance of self-awareness and how a deeper understanding of yourself provides you with important and useful information to understand the signs you identified in Stage 1. Self-awareness is also instrumental to your ability to create a vision and plan for change that is authentic to you, your values, and your personal experiences. In **Stage 3: Design Your Vision**, you learned how to take the work you did in Stages 1 and 2 and apply it to designing a vision for your future. In **Stage 4: Create the Plan**, you learned what was required to develop a plan to make your vision a reality. You learned about identifying and prioritizing end goals and creating milestones and action steps that are useful in helping you succeed. In **Stage 5: Make It Happen**, you learned the importance of proper execution of your plan, the types of obstacles you might encounter as you try to make changes, and how to overcome these obstacles. You also learned how to stay motivated, how to modify habits so they are healthier and more productive, and how to identify ways to create more consistent behaviors so that changes are more apt to stick. And finally, in **Stage 6: Monitor Your Progress**, you learned about the importance of revisiting your plan often to evaluate what is working and what isn't, and how you can revise it to make it more effective.

All the stages presented are instrumental to your ability to create a wonderful, happy life, and will help you make positive change so that you can be your best. The process applies to any type of change or reinvention you want to go through, regardless of the dimension or dimensions of well-being you are concerned about. No matter your age or where you are in life, this process will work. If you give it the time and energy it deserves, you can make whatever changes you want and achieve the happiness that you wish.

Use this book as your guide throughout the many personal reinventions you may experience during your lifetime, and best of luck creating the life you desire. You deserve it.

Part III

THE NEW YOU JOURNAL

STAGE 1: IDENTIFY THE NEED

DIMENSIONS OF WELL-BEING SELF-ASSESSMENT

Dimensions	Importance	Satisfaction
Career Well-Being		
Physical Well-Being		
Social Well-Being		
Emotional Well-Being		
Intellectual Well-Being		
Spiritual Well-Being		

THE PERSONAL SIGNS OF CHANGE MATRIX

Dimensions	Rational Signs	Physical Signs	Emotional Signs
Career Well-Being			
Social Well-Being			
Intellectual Well-Being			
Physical Well-Being			
Emotional Well-Being			
Spiritual Well-Being			

RATIONAL AND EMOTIONAL SOS ASSESSMENT

Dimensions	Emotional Signs of Significance	Possible Cause
Career Well-Being		
Social Well-Being		
Intellectual Well-Being		
Physical Well-Being		
Emotional Well-Being		
Spiritual Well-Being		

Physical SOS Assessment

Physical Signs of Significance	When SOS Occurs	Possible Dimension of Well-Being

STAGE 2: DISCOVER YOURSELF

My Values Worksheet

Values	Rating	Values	Rating

MY MOST IMPORTANT VALUES WORKSHEET

My Most Important Values	Ranking

Core Values

_____

_____

_____

_____

_____

MY STRENGTHS WORKSHEET

Dimensions	Strengths	Examples
Career Well-Being		
Social Well-Being		
Intellectual Well-Being		
Physical Well-Being		
Emotional Well-Being		
Spiritual Well-Being		

My Weaknesses Worksheet

Dimensions	Weaknesses to Avoid
Career Well-Being	
Social Well-Being	
Intellectual Well-Being	
Physical Well-Being	
Emotional Well-Being	
Spiritual Well-Being	

MY PAST FEARS WORKSHEET

Past Fears	Emotions	Reality	Control

A New Story of an Old Fear

_____

_____

_____

_____

_____

My Current Fears Worksheet

Current Fears	Control	What I Can Do

A Story of a Forgotten Fear

_____

_____

_____

_____

_____

MY CONQUERED FEARS WORKSHEET

Conquered Fears	Cause	What I Did	Outcome

A Story of a Conquered Fear

_____

_____

_____

_____

_____

MY PASSIONS WORKSHEET

Passion	How It Makes Me Feel	How Can I Tap into This?

MY ACCOMPLISHMENTS WORKSHEET

Accomplishment	The Way I Felt	The Time It Took	The Steps I Took

LESSONS LEARNED

MY FAILURES WORKSHEET

Failures	Lessons Learned	Positive Impact

My Motivators Worksheet

Core Values	Motivators

My Upbringing Worksheet

How would I rate my overall happiness level at home?

_____

What was my family's structure like, and how did I feel about it?

_____

_____

_____

_____

_____

What were each family member's positive attributes, negative attributes, and my relationship with them?

_____

_____

_____

_____

How did I feel about my home life as a child? As a teenager? As a young adult? Today?

_____

_____

What did I like most about my upbringing?

_____

_____

_____

What did I like least about my upbringing?

_____

_____

_____

What would I change if I could?

_____

_____

_____

My Life Experiences Worksheet

How did I feel outside the home as a child? As a teenager? As a young adult?

_____

_____

_____

_____

What were my experiences in grade school like? In high school? In college?

_____

_____

_____

_____

What activities did I get involved in? Did I enjoy them?

_____

_____

_____

_____

How have these experiences shaped me as a person?

_____

_____

_____

How would I describe my work experiences?

_____

_____

_____

What five experiences have provided me the greatest pleasure? Why?

_____

_____

_____

What experiences have I had that caused me the greatest pain or hurt? Why?

_____

_____

_____

My Combined Experiences Worksheet

What experiences outside of the home required my parents or other family members' reactions or involvement?

_____

_____

_____

What were their reactions? How did they behave toward me? Toward the situation? Toward the other individuals involved?

_____

_____

_____

How do I feel about their reactions or how they handled the situation?

_____

_____

_____

How has any of this shaped my life and who I am today?

_____

_____

_____

THE WHAT I WANT WORKSHEET

What do I hope I will have accomplished in my lifetime?

_____

_____

_____

What would I want my child to think of me? My grandchildren?

_____

_____

_____

What would I want my eulogy to say?

_____

_____

_____

What would bring me the most pleasure, fulfillment, contentment, and satisfaction?

_____

_____

_____

MY MISSION STATEMENT WORKSHEET

What characteristics and qualities do I want to live by?

_____

_____

_____

How do I want to contribute to the world?

_____

_____

_____

What kind of influence do I want to have?

_____

_____

_____

What legacy would I like to leave?

_____

_____

_____

_____

_____

STAGE 3: DESIGN YOUR VISION

THE PERSONAL REINVENTION GAP MAP

Today

Tomorrow

MY IDEAL TOMORROW WORKSHEET

What would my ideal life look like?

_____

_____

_____

_____

_____

_____

_____

_____

_____

_____

_____

_____

_____

MY VISION WORKSHEET

Vision Statement Draft:

_____

_____

_____

_____

_____

_____

_____

_____

_____

My Vision Statement for Personal Reinvention:

_____

_____

_____

_____

Vision Effectiveness Evaluation

Evaluation	Yes	No
Will this vision push me beyond today?		
Is it attainable and realistic?		
Will achieving this vision make me happier?		
Is it clear and simple?		
Will I continue to be inspired by this vision?		
Is it measurable?		
Is it consistent with my values and my mission statement?		
Is it authentic to me?		
Is it achievable within a one- to five-year time frame?		
Does this resonate with me? Do I like this vision?		

STAGE 4: CREATE THE PLAN

THE BIG END GOALS WORKSHEET

#	End Goals	SMARTE Criteria	Key Requirements	Impact	Difficulty	Priority
1						
2						
3						
4						
5						
6						
7						
8						
9						

THE PRIORITIZATION MATRIX WORKSHEET

The Prioritization Matrix

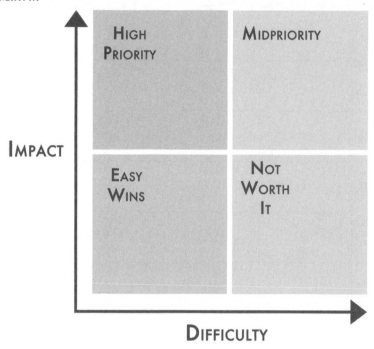

Prioritized End Goals

1		6	
2		7	
3		8	
4		9	
5		10	

THE END GOALS, MILESTONES, AND ACTION STEPS WORKSHEET

End Goals	Milestones		Action Steps	Due Date	Reward
_____	1 _____	1a	_____	_____	_____
		1b	_____	_____	_____
		1c	_____	_____	_____
		1d	_____	_____	_____
		1e	_____	_____	_____
			Milestone Due Date	_____	
	2 _____	2a	_____	_____	_____
		2b	_____	_____	_____
		2c	_____	_____	_____
		2d	_____	_____	_____
		2e	_____	_____	_____
			Milestone Due Date	_____	
	3 _____	3a	_____	_____	_____
		3b	_____	_____	_____
		3c	_____	_____	_____
		3d	_____	_____	_____
		3e	_____	_____	_____
			Milestone Due Date	_____	
	4 _____	4a	_____	_____	_____
		4b	_____	_____	_____
		4c	_____	_____	_____
		4d	_____	_____	_____
		4e	_____	_____	_____
			Milestone Due Date	_____	_____

END GOAL DUE DATE _____ _____

STAGE 5: MAKE IT HAPPEN

The List of Affirmations Worksheet

DUHIGG'S HABIT LOOP MODIFICATION WORKSHEET

CURRENT HABIT LOOP

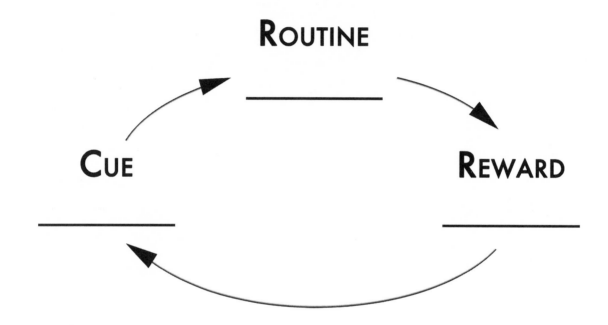

What Needs to Change

_____

_____

Opportunities for Modification

_____

_____

THE NEW HABIT LOOP

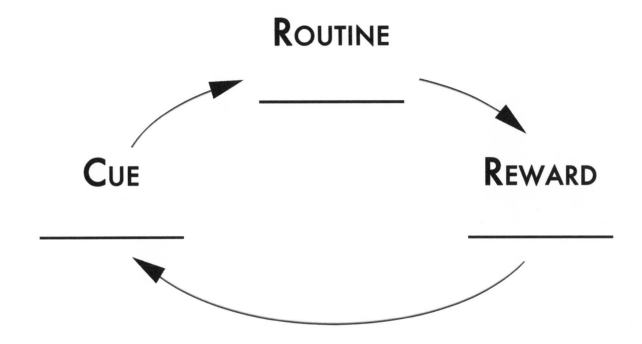

ROUTINE

CUE

REWARD

THE INCONSISTENT BEHAVIORS WORKSHEET

Results of Change

_____

_____

_____

_____

Inconsistencies

_____

_____

_____

_____

Moments of Consistency

_____

_____

_____

_____

My Failures of Reinvention Worksheet

Failures	Causes	Lessons Learned	Moving Forward

STAGE 6: MONITOR YOUR PROGRESS

The Checkpoint Evaluation Worksheet

Evaluation	Yes	No
Am I making progress toward the upcoming milestone or goal?		
Am I staying true to my vision, values, and mission statement?		
Do I feel comfortable with and in control of my current action steps?		
Do they feel realistic?		
Am I motivated to continue forward?		
Is everything working well in the plan?		

How It's Going

_____

_____

_____

_____

RESOURCES

Regardless of the dimensions of well-being you are focusing on, there are many wonderful books and resources that address the topic of change. Here's a list of some of my personal favorites.

General Well-Being

- Duhigg, Charles. *The Power of Habit: Why We Do What We Do in Life and Business*. New York: Random House, 2012.

- Dweck, Carol S. *Mindset: The New Psychology of Success*. New York: Ballantine Books, 2008.

- Heath, Chip, and Dan Heath. *Switch: How to Change Things When Change Is Hard*. New York: Broadway Books, 2010.

- Kotter, John P. *Leading Change*. Harvard Business Review Press, 1st edition (January 15, 1996).

Career Well-Being

- Buckingham, Marcus. *StandOut: The Groundbreaking New Strengths Assessment from the Leader of the Strengths Revolution*. Nashville, TN: Thomas Nelson, 2011.

- Miedaner, Talane. *Coach Yourself to a New Career: 7 Steps to Reinventing Your Professional Life*. New York: McGraw-Hill, 2010.

- Mitchell, Pamela. *The 10 Laws of Career Reinvention: Essential Survival Skills for Any Economy*. New York: Dutton, 2010.

Social Well-Being

- Bradberry, Travis, and Jean Greaves. *Emotional Intelligence 2.0*. San Diego: TalentSmart, 2009.

- Covey, Stephen R. *The 7 Habits of Highly Effective People*. New York: Free Press, 2004.

Emotional Well-Being

- Davidson, Richard J., and Sharon Begley. *The Emotional Life of Your Brain: How Its Unique Patterns Affect the Way You Think, Feel, and Live—And How You Can Change Them*. London: Hudson Street Press, 2012.

- Johnson, L. Whitney. *Dare, Dream, Do: Remarkable Things Happen When You Dare to Dream*. Brookline: Bibliomotion, 2012.

- LaPorte, Danielle. *The Fire Starter Sessions: A Soulful + Practical Guide to Creating Success on Your Own Terms*. New York: Crown Archetype, 2012.

- Rubin, Gretchen. *The Happiness Project: Or, Why I Spent a Year Trying to Sing in the Morning, Clean My Closets, Fight Right, Read Aristotle, and Generally Have More Fun*. New York: HarperCollins, 2009.

- Seligman, Martin E. P. *Authentic Happiness: Using the New Positive Psychology to Realize Your Potential for Lasting Fulfillment*. New York: Free Press, 2002.

Physical Well-Being

- Blumenthal, Brett. *52 Small Changes: One Year to a Happier, Healthier You*. Seattle: AmazonEncore, 2011.

- Lauren, Mark, and Joshua Clark. *You Are Your Own Gym: The Bible of Bodyweight Exercises*. New York: Ballantine Books, 2011.

- Taubes, Gary. *Good Calories, Bad Calories: Fats, Carbs, and the Controversial Science of Diet and Health.* New York: Anchor Books, 2008.

- Wansink, Brian. *Mindless Eating: Why We Eat More Than We Think.* New York: Bantam Books, 2010.

INTELLECTUAL WELL-BEING

- Carson, Shelley. *Your Creative Brain: Seven Steps to Maximize Imagination, Productivity, and Innovation in Your Life.* Harvard Health Publications. San Francisco: Jossey-Bass, 2010.

- Moore, Margaret, and Paul Hammerness, with John Hanc. *Organize Your Mind, Organize Your Life: Train Your Brain to Get More Done in Less Time.* Don Mills, ON: Harlequin, 2011.

- Rock, David. *Your Brain at Work: Strategies for Overcoming Distraction, Regaining Focus, and Working Smarter All Day Long.* New York: HarperCollins, 2009.

SPIRITUAL WELL-BEING

- Chopra, Deepak. *The Ultimate Happiness Prescription: 7 Keys to Joy and Enlightenment.* New York: Harmony Books, 2009.

- Haidt, Jonathan. *The Happiness Hypothesis: Finding Modern Truth in Ancient Wisdom.* New York: Basic Books, 2006.

- Kabat-Zinn, Jon. *Mindfulness for Beginners: Reclaiming the Present Moment—And Your Life.* Boulder, CO: Sounds True, 2012.

ACKNOWLEDGMENTS

I WOULD LIKE TO EXPRESS MY sincere thanks to all the individuals who have contributed to making *A Whole New You* the best book possible.

Thank you to my agents Meg Thompson and Sandy Hodgman for stepping in and running with the ball without missing a beat. To my editor, Carmen Johnson, thank you for jumping in with two feet and providing your guidance, insight, and honesty. Your commitment to making tight timelines a reality has been greatly appreciated. Thank you to the team at Amazon Publishing, including Alexandra Woodworth, Alicia Criner, and Elizabeth Johnson for your time, dedication, and support in this project, and for being with me every step of the way through editing, design, marketing, and publicity.

Thank you to Lucinda Blumenfeld, my publicist, for being my champion, cheerleader, and advocate throughout this process. Having you in my corner has been wonderful.

Thank you to all the individuals who have opened their hearts and shared their stories about their fears, challenges, passions, and personal reinventions: Jane Chow, Tamara Davies Christie, Debra Cohen, Sam Davis, Carole Brody Fleet, Kristi Jade, Elizabeth Jansen, Tobi Kosanke, Andy LaPointe, Lisa Lewis, Kimberly Miller, Joy Weese Moll, Elizabeth Sandman, Susan Schenck, John Simmons, and Philip Wax.

Thank you to all the wonderful authors and writers who, unbeknownst to them, have had an influence on this book and me: Marcus Buckingham, Donald O. Clifton, Stephen R. Covey, Charles Duhigg, Carol Dweck, Chip Heath, Dan Heath, Napoleon Hill, John P. Kotter, and Gretchen Rubin.

Finally, thank you to David for your unwavering belief in my work and in us. And thank you to Mom and Bill for always encouraging me to be my best, every day.

ABOUT THE AUTHOR

 Brett Blumenthal is the best-selling author of *52 Small Changes: One Year to a Happier, Healthier You,* and *Get Real and Stop Dieting!* She has over twenty years of experience in wellness, and almost ten years in management consulting, advising Fortune 100 companies on managing change within their organizations. Brett received her MBA, as well as her bachelor's degree, from Cornell University. She is certified by the Wellness Council of America (WELCOA) and the Aerobics and Fitness Association of America (AFAA).